Georg Wolf's
Electric Guitar Basics

Voggenreiter

The original songs published in this book are protected by copyright.
Reprint only with the express permission from authorised parties.

All rights to the compilation of this book are held by
VOGGENREITER VERLAG

Cover: OZ, Essen (Katrin & Christian Brackmann)
Assembly & layout: B&O

© 2006 VOGGENREITER VERLAG
Viktoriastr. 25, D-53173 Bonn
www.voggenreiter.de
Telephone: +49 228 / 93 575-0

ISBN 978-3-8024-0607-2

Foreword

A cheery hello and hearty welcome to *Electric Guitar Basics*!

With the aid of this guitar course you should be able to achieve a position from which you can begin a career as a guitarist. Whether you currently wish to play in a band, to use the guitar as an accompaniment to your singing abilities or to create a melody on this wonderful instrument: You should obtain the foundations upon which to achieve your ambitions right here.

In addition to an introduction to the harmonies and various strumming techniques used in accompanying songs, this book should also provide the basis for playing in single notes. In view of the fact that one has improved chances of development if one is not only competent at playing, but also possesses an understanding of the fundamental musical contexts, this book also contains an exercise-based theory section.

The enclosed CD is intended for use either as a playing aid or exercise guide, and may also provide motivational support. However keep one thought in focus: Playing should be fun.

Enjoy yourself!
Georg Wolf

CONTENTS

Part 1

1. MY INSTRUMENT 6
   The guitar 6
   Playing Position 7
      Relaxed playing position 7
      Standing playing position 7
      Classic playing position 7
   Tuning 8

2. FROM THE FIRST CHORDS TO THE FIRST SONG 9
   The chord diagram 9
   The first two chords 10
   Strumming technique 11
   Time signature 11
   Our first song:
      JOSHUA FIT THE BATTLE OF JERICHO 12
   Major and minor 12

3. MORE CHORDS - AN EXTENDED REPERTOIRE 13
   E minor and D major 13
   The second song:
      WHAT SHALL WE DO WITH THE DRUNKEN SAILOR 13
   This is how it sounds with 3 chords:
      ADVENTURE IS STILL CALLING 14
   D minor and A major 14
   The next songs:
      WAKING UP IN WONDERLAND 15
      GO DOWN, MOSES 15
      SWING LOW, SWEET CHARIOT 15

4. STRUMMING ON 16
   Stop and Go 16
   The G major chord:
      CORINNA 16
   3/4 time:
      MY BONNIE IS OVER THE OCEAN 17

5. THE DOMINANT SEVENTH CHORD 17
   The B^7 chord:
      IT´S ME, OH LORD 18
   Dominant seventh chords G, D, A and E 18
   Additional strumming technique in 2/4 time 20
      SHE´LL BE COMIN´ ROUND THE MOUNTAIN 20
   C major and C^7 chord 20
      SOMETIMES I FEEL LIKE A MOTHERLESS CHILD 21

6. BARRE - WITH NO BARRIERS 22
   The F major chord:
      BACKWATER BLUES 22
   6/8 time 23
      HOUSE OF THE RISING SUN 23
   Two main barre types 23
   The E type 23
   The A type 24
   The powerchord 26
   The combination of powerchords and harmonies 26

  THE FIRE IN YOUR EYES 26
  The riff from the song MAKE ME MOVE 27

Part 2

7. PLAYING SINGLE NOTES 28
 Positioning your hands 28
 Picking technique 29
 The open strings 29
 The notes on the G string 30
 The notes on the B string 31
  OH, WHEN THE SAINTS 32
 The notes on the E string 32
  DOWN IN THE VALLEY 33
 The notes on the D string 33
 The notes on the A string 34
  I CAN´T BELIEVE IT 35
 The notes on the E string 35
  TOM DOOLEY 36
  JOHN BROWN´S BODY 36
 The notes with ♯ and ♭ 37
 Tablature notation 37
 Accompanying songs with chords 39

Part 3

8. MUSICAL NOTATION 41
 The staves 41
 The names of the notes 41
 The clef 42
 The octaves 42
 The note values 43
 The dot and the tie 44
 The rests 44
 The triplet 45
 The accidentals 45
 Bars 46
 The anacrusis (upbeat) 48
 Syncopation 48
 The repeat sign 48
 The fermata 49

9. THE CIRCLE OF FIFTHS 50
 The major scale 50
 The major circle of fifths 52
 Accidentals 53
 The minor scales 53
 The minor circle of fifths 54

10. THE CHORDS 55
 Intervals 55
 The tritone 55
 Enharmonic exchange 55
 Chord construction 56
 Chord inversions 57
 The seventh chord 57
 The chord names 59
 CD-Tracklist 61
 Chord diagrams 62

MY INSTRUMENT

THE GUITAR

- Headstock
- Tuning pegs
- Neck
- Frets
- Body
- Pickup
- Vibrato
- Pickup selector
- Volume & tone controls
- Bridge
- Output jack

Individual operating elements may vary, depending upon the specific instrument selected.

PLAYING POSITION

Relaxed playing position

Many guitarists prefer holding the guitar whilst sitting, if they are practising for any length of time. You can simply rest the guitar on the right thigh and support it with the right arm. If you wish to cross your legs, simply place the guitar on the top leg.

Relaxed playing position

Standing playing position

Rock and pop music pieces in particular are usually played on the guitar held in a standing hold, with the aid of a guitar strap. Make sure that the instrument does not hang down too low or you may experience problems when holding down the chords. If you are not able to attach a strap to your guitar then clamp the instrument using the crook of your arm and your upper body. This position will require some practise.

Standing playing position

Classic playing position

Sit yourself towards the front half of your stool and place your left foot on a footrest. Place the guitar on your left upper thigh so that your leg fits naturally into the curvature of the body. You can use your right leg to keep the instrument in position.

The same applies to all holding variations:
You should remain loose and relaxed for playing!

Classic playing position

TUNING

The names of the strings from the thickest to the thinnest are:

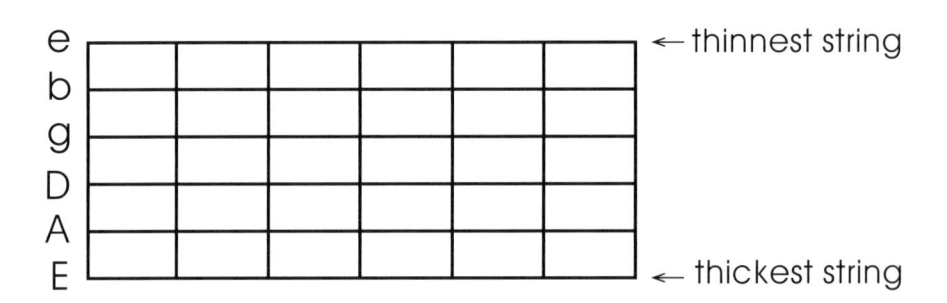

```
e  ──┬───┬───┬───┬───┬───┬──  ← thinnest string
b  ──┼───┼───┼───┼───┼───┼──
g  ──┼───┼───┼───┼───┼───┼──
D  ──┼───┼───┼───┼───┼───┼──
A  ──┼───┼───┼───┼───┼───┼──
E  ──┴───┴───┴───┴───┴───┴──  ← thickest string
```

The easiest method of tuning the guitar is to use an **electronic tuner**.
Further tuning possibilities are provided by other sources of notes (keyboard instruments, pitch pipes), or with the aid of a **tuning fork**.

The guitar can be tuned as follows using a tuning fork (standard musical pitch A):
You raise the A string to the requisite pitch.
The note A, which you obtain on the E string at the 5th fret, is matched with the sound of the open (untouched) A string.

After this the following are matched:

Open D string with the A string held at 5th fret
Open g string with the D string held at 5th fret
Open b string with the g string held at 4th fret
Open e string with the b string held at 5th fret

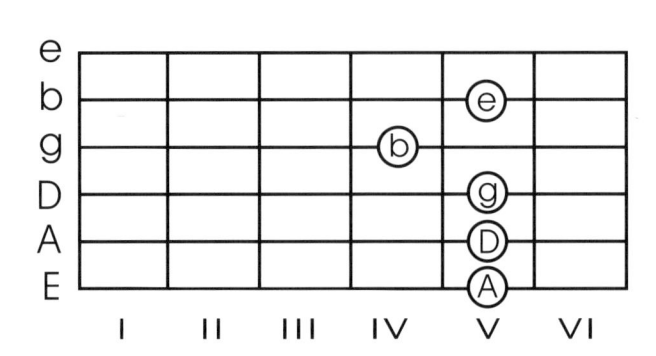

FROM THE FIRST CHORDS TO THE FIRST SONG

THE CHORD DIAGRAM

The chord is held down using the left hand (fretting hand) which is placed on the fretboard, on the neck of the guitar.
In order to demonstrate which fingers should be used in each case we number them as follows:

Index finger   =   1
Middle finger =   2
Ring finger   =   3
Little finger =   4

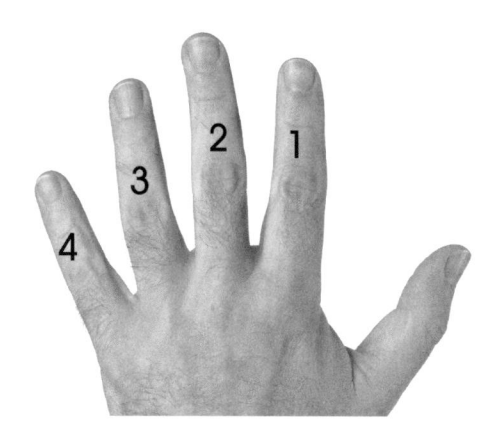

The thumb serves to provide support to the rear side of the guitar neck. A small cross to the left of the chord diagram denotes an empty string which should also be strummed; strings which should not be strummed, or which should be damped, are recognised by an "x". The chord diagram depicts the fretboard with the fret distribution and the position of the fingers.

THE FIRST TWO CHORDS

Our first chord is known as A minor (in short Am) (see music theory).

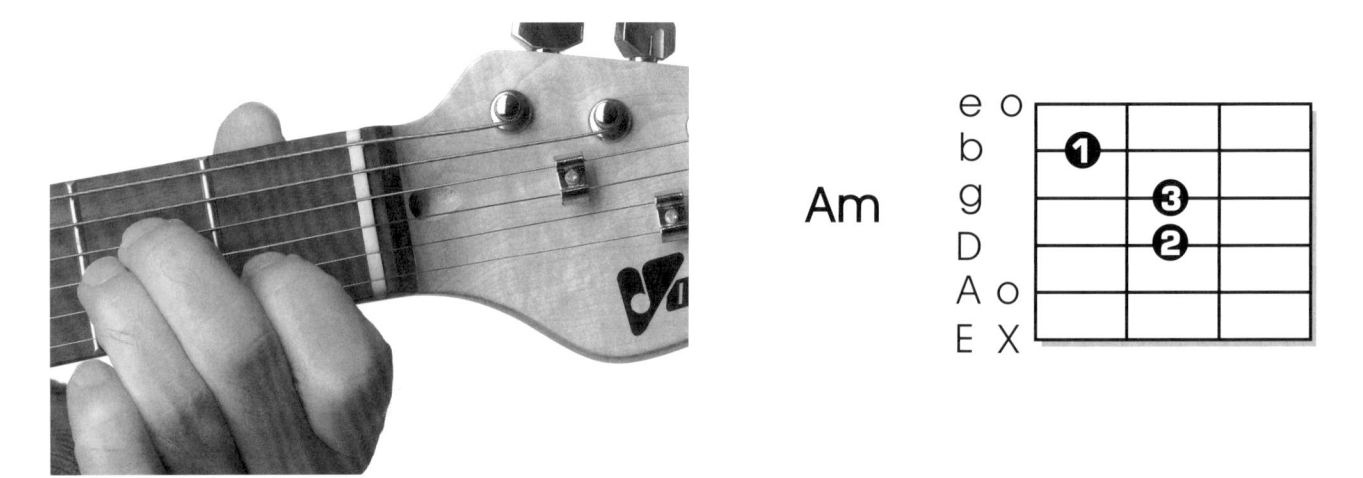

Place the fingers vertically over the strings and strum each of them in turn using the thumb of your right hand, in order to check the clarity of sound.

Ensure that your fretting hand is not closed too tightly around the guitar neck and that you are not applying too much pressure.

The hold for our second chord, E major (in short E), is similar to that of Am.

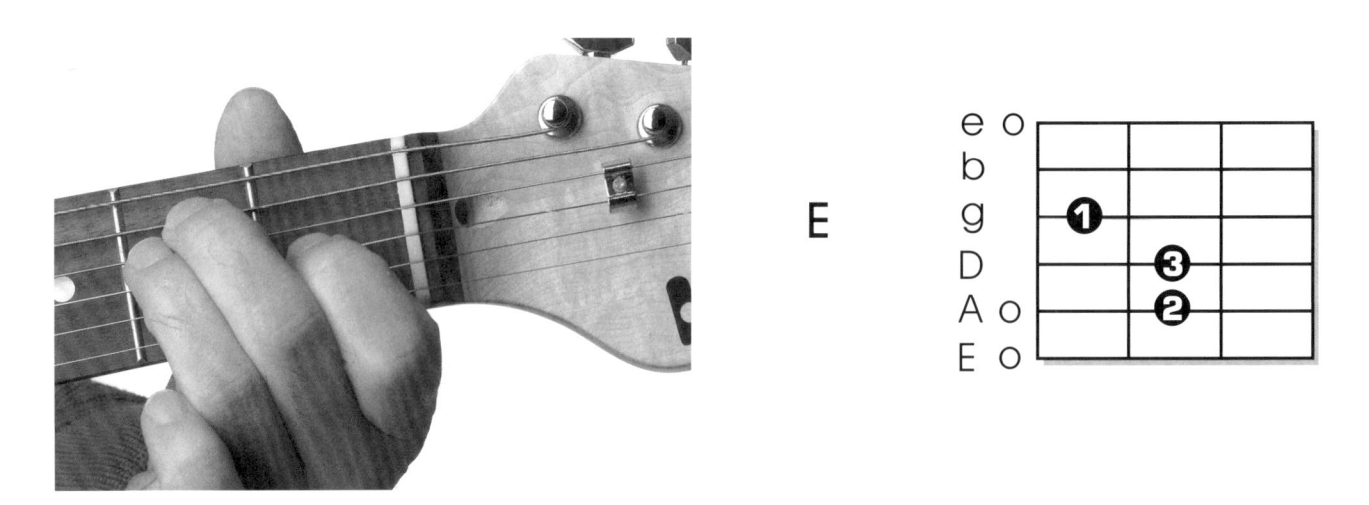

Again, check the sound clarity of each string when holding down this chord.

STRUMMING TECHNIQUE

You can strum the chords with the fingers of your right hand (picking hand) or by using a **plectrum** or **pick** held between the thumb and index finger.

Plectrum (pick)

For the remainder of the book, all chords will be strummed using a plectrum.

We differentiate between two strumming directions:
From the thickest to the thinnest string = **downstroke** (symbol ⊓)
From the thinnest to the thickest string = **upstroke** (symbol V)

Even downstroke and upstroke movements, which should be produced from the wrist, will create the rhythm.

Hold down the Am chord and practise the downstroke and upstroke motions.
Also try this with E.

TIME SIGNATURE

Every piece of music is divided into equal sections by **bar lines**. These sections are known as **bars** (see music theory).
Two numbers are displayed at the start of a piece of music showing the time signature. The **top** one denotes the number of equal beats in each bar, whilst the **bottom** number informs us of the **value**, in time, of each beat.
If for example we see 4/4 behind the clef (see music theory) then this tells us that every bar will comprise of four beats, and that the value of each beat is a quarter note, or a crotchet.
The first song that we want to learn is played in 4/4 time.

OUR FIRST SONG:
JOSHUA FIT THE BATTLE OF JERICHO

In order to play the hymn "Joshua fit the battle of Jericho", you will need the two chords Am and E. Below you can see the chord pattern:

Joshua fit the battle of Jericho

Chorus $\frac{4}{4}$ |Am|Am| E |Am|Am|Am| E |Am|

Verse |Am| E |Am| E |Am|Am| E |Am|

First practise the song by strumming 4 downstrokes in each bar. You will almost certainly take a little time to change chord initially. Try to constantly reduce the pauses which occur during each change, until there is no pause at all.
One more tip: It is easier if you simply "set" your hand in position, in other words move and place all fingers at the same time. "Rolling" the fingers (moving and placing each one in turn) requires too much time!

Once you have the feeling that you are able to play the chords with rhythm, play each in the sequence chorus – verse – chorus with the accompaniment. Instead of strumming 4 times on each chord in a downstroke, we shall now attempt to play downstrokes and upstrokes in alternation.

The continuous rhythm requires that you keep up with the accompaniment, making difficulties when changing chords highly audible.

Remain patient and keep trying (with and without the accompaniment)! Every pupil requires time to train the fingers to move in this unusual way. This also applies to the following exercises.

MAJOR AND MINOR

The terms "major" and "minor" are the names for the two modes in music. **Major**, the hard mode, is considered a light and cheerful sound, whilst the **soft minor** is considered melancholy and sad.
If you wish to know more about this subject take a look in the music theory section.

MORE CHORDS - AN EXTENDED REPERTOIRE

E MINOR AND D MAJOR

The E minor chord (in short Em) is one of the simplest chords on the guitar, because you only need to hold down 2 fingers. **Tip**: Hold down E and lift the 1st finger out of the way!

When playing the D major chord (in short D) ensure that you do not also strum the E and A strings.

Practise both chords individually and then alternate between the two.

THE SECOND SONG:
WHAT SHALL WE DO WITH THE DRUNKEN SAILOR

Using Em and D we can play an English sailor's song: "What shall we do with the drunken sailor". The song is played in 2/4 time; in other words there are two downstrokes or one downstroke and one upstroke per bar.

What shall we do with the drunken sailor

$\frac{2}{4}$ | Em | Em | D | D | Em | Em | D | Em |

| Em | Em | D | D | Em | Em | D | Em |

The change from E to Dm is certainly more difficult to master than that between Am and E. Take your time before playing along with the accompaniment.

THIS IS HOW IT SOUNDS WITH 3 CHORDS:
ADVENTURE IS STILL CALLING

Once you have learned the two songs with 2 chords in them, the following song, with its 3 chords, will be no problem for you: "Adventure is still calling".

Adventure is still calling

$\frac{4}{4}$ |Am| D |Am| E |Am| D |Am E |Am|

The second to last bar is harmoniously divided in two. You strum twice in Am and twice in E. You will need to practise the change from Am to D. And now it's time to enjoy the Wild West!

D MINOR AND A MAJOR

We shall now extend our skills to include a further two chords.
First of all, D minor (in short Dm):

Dm

As previously learned with D, we do not strum the last two strings. A major (in short A) is well loved by all guitarists, because the position of the fingers is one which comes very naturally.

A

14

THE NEXT SONGS:
WAKING UP IN WONDERLAND
GO DOWN, MOSES
SWING LOW, SWEET CHARIOT

Once you have mastered playing the two chords, Dm and A, and are able to change between them well, we shall continue by playing the song "Waking up in wonderland", the chord pattern for which is shown below.

Waking up in wonderland

$\frac{4}{4}$ |Dm| A |Dm| A |Dm| A |Dm A|Dm|

In order to gain further playing practise, we will continue by studying the next two hymns. Firstly the piece "Go down, Moses", which begins with an incomplete opening bar, which forms a complete bar when added together with the equally incomplete closing bar (see music theory). However this closing bar is not always observed, in particular in pop and rock music. In the following song the opening bar is performed by a solo instrument. We come in with the guitar on the first beat of the first complete bar.

Go down, Moses

$\frac{4}{4}$ ♩|Am E |Am| E |Am|Am E |Am| E |Am|

|Am|Dm|Am E |Am|Dm|Am| E |Am|

The second song is called "Swing low, sweet chariot".

Swing low, sweet chariot

$\frac{4}{4}$| A |D A| A | E | A |D A|A E| A |

| A |D A| A | E | A |D A|A E| A |

STRUMMING ON

STOP AND GO

In order to achieve more drive in our playing we will start to work with a new strumming pattern.
Up to now, we have played in 4/4 time with 4 downstrokes (⊓⊓⊓⊓) or with alternating downstrokes and upstrokes (⊓V⊓V). Now, when we strum four times we shall be adding one more downstroke and one more upstroke:

⊓ V ⊓ V ⊓ V ⊓ V

1 + ② + 3 + ④ +

If you count out loud whilst you play, you will announce a number with every downstroke and an "and" with every upstroke that follows.
The numbers 2 and 4, circled on the diagram, are used as percussion beats. The strings are dampened either during or immediately after strumming. Do this using the side of your picking hand: One calls this action "stopping".

Practise this strumming pattern slowly at first, so that you become confident when moving your picking hand in this unusual way. You will become faster with experience. Now try to select a different chord for each bar, making sure that there is no break in the rhythm during chord changes. Keep playing with your picking hand, even if the chord positions are not quite perfect.

THE G MAJOR CHORD:
CORINNA

Our next chord is called G major (in short G). As you can see from the chord diagram, you can strum across all strings when playing this chord.

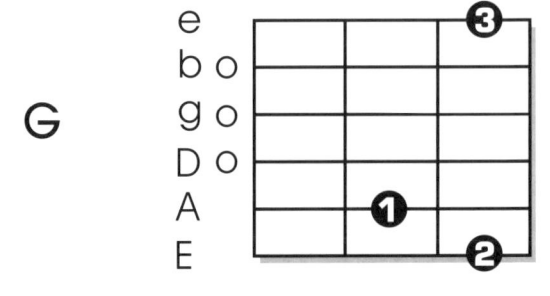

16

The next song requires a little initial preparation:
Play the chord sequence | D | G | D | A | many times in succession and use the new strumming technique at the same time, with the percussion beat. Once you have mastered this harmony sequence you can play the following piece "Corinna" without trouble.

Corinna

$\frac{4}{4}$ ₹ - | D | D | D | D | G | G | D | D |

| A | A | D | A |

| D | D | D | D | G | G | D | D |

| A | A | D | D |

3/4 TIME:
MY BONNIE IS OVER THE OCEAN

The first **odd time signature** (see music theory) that we wish to learn is 3/4 time. It is divided into one upstroke and two downstrokes of the picking hand (V▬▬).

Practise the harmony sequence | A | D | A | E | in preparation for the next song "My Bonnie is over the ocean".

My Bonnie is over the ocean

$\frac{3}{4}$ ₹ | D | G | D | D | D | E | A | A | D | G | D | D | G | A | D | D |

| D | D | G | E | A | A | D | D | D | D | G | E | A | A | D | D |

THE DOMINANT SEVENTH CHORD

The major and minor chords that we have played thus far each comprise of the 1st, 3rd and 5th note on the respective scale.
If one adds the diminished seventh note (see music theory) then one creates a four note sound: The **dominant seventh chord**. If this type of chord is required in a piece then this is indicated with the addition of a superscript "7" after the chord symbol (e.g. B^7 or G^7).

THE B⁷ CHORD:
IT'S ME, OH LORD

Our first dominant seventh chord is not quite so easy to hold down: B⁷ is one of the most difficult basic guitar chord positions.

B⁷

Practise the exercise | E | H⁷ | E | H⁷ | sfor as long as necessary, until you are able to change between the chords smoothly and without a break in rhythm. Only then will it be possible for you to play the hymn "It's me, oh Lord".

It's me, oh Lord

$\frac{4}{4}$ ₹ | E |B⁷ E |E B⁷| E | E |B⁷ E |E B⁷| E |

| E |B⁷ E |A B⁷| E | E |B⁷ E |A B⁷| E |

DOMINANT SEVENTH CHORDS G, D, A AND E

The following chord diagrams show the dominant seventh chord versions of the major chords that we have learned so far.
You will need to adopt a completely new position for the G⁷ and D⁷ chords from that of their major chord variants.

G⁷

18

Part 1

D⁷

In the case of A⁷ and E⁷ the basic position remains the same, with the added use of the little finger for the new note.

A⁷

E⁷

In order to practise E⁷ listen once more to our first songs "Joshua fit the battle of Jericho" or "Go down, Moses" and then play E⁷ in place of the E chord.

19

ADDITIONAL STRUMMING TECHNIQUE IN 2/4 TIME

The two dominant seventh chords of D and A are both found in the song "She'll be coming' round the mountain". The piece is played in 2/4 time, a time signature that we saw earlier in "What shall we do with the drunken sailor". In this case, the pickin hand plays four downstrokes per bar. One essentially counts 4 1/8th notes (quavers), whereby 1+ and 2+ are played as stops:

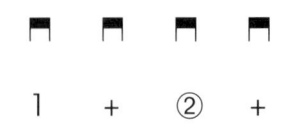

1   +   ②   +

She'll be comin' round the mountain

$\frac{2}{4}$ 𝄽 𝄽 | D | D | D | D | D | D | A | A |

| D | D | G | G | D | A | D | D |

We have now practised the chords D^7, A^7 and E^7 whilst playing. We now shall practise the G^7 chord together with C major in the next section.

C MAJOR AND THE C^7 CHORD

We are now going to look at the last of the so-called "simple basic chords", C major and C^7. The position for C^7 is similar to that of G^7.

C

Practise C and G⁷ in alternation: | C | G⁷ | C | G⁷ |

In order to play "Sometimes I feel like a motherless child" we will need to use a new strumming technique, which is particularly well suited to accompanying slower songs in 4/4 time:

⊓ ⊓ V ⊓ V ⊓ ⊓ V ⊓ V

1e + e 2e +e 3e + e 4e +e

Counting time is once again divided by adding an "**and**" between strokes 1 and 3. One says "and-e".
Hold down a chord and practise the new strumming technique first. Now we are ready to play "Sometimes I feel like a motherless child".

Sometimes I feel like a motherless child 🔘11

$\frac{4}{4}$ |Em |Em |Am| Em| Em| Em |C Em |B⁷ Em| C B⁷ |Em B⁷|

|Em |Em |Am| Em| Em| Em |C Em |B⁷ Em| C B⁷ | Em |

The C7 chord

As with A7 and E⁷ we only need to add the little finger to the major chord to play C⁷.

C⁷

BARRE - WITH NO BARRIERS

THE F MAJOR CHORD:
BACKWATER BLUES

The so-called barre chords require that the index finger on the fretting hand be laid right across the guitar strings. The finger acts in place of the nut.
One requires a good deal of time and patience to hold down the first barre chord correctly whilst also gaining a good sound. But don't panic! Something that might initially sound like a car crash will soon become a great sound with practise.

Let us start with F major (in short F).

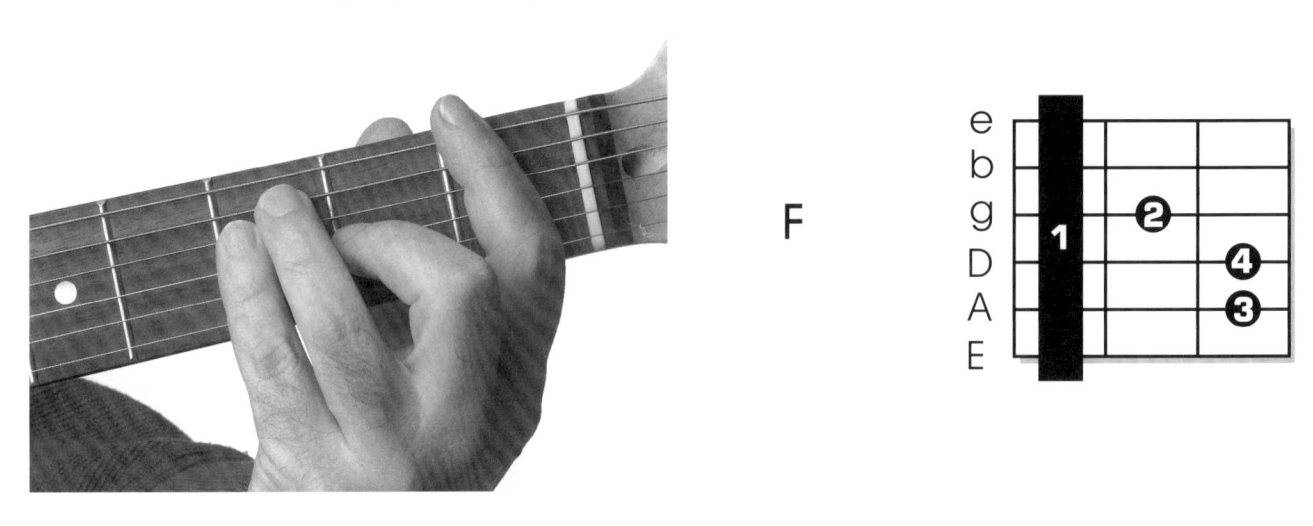

F

In order to practise we shall play the chord sequence | C C^7 | F | C G^7 | C | a number of times over. Once you are holding down F with some confidence we can have a go at "Backwater Blues".

Backwater Blues

$\frac{4}{4}$ ɣ ɣ | C^7 | F | C | C^7 | F | F | C | C^7 | G^7 | F | C | G^7 |

| C^7 | F | C | C^7 | F | F | C | C^7 | G^7 | F | C | C |

6/8 TIME

In order to be able to play in 6/8 time we require the following strumming pattern:

▀ ▀ V ▀ ▀ ▀ ▀

1 2 + 3 4 5 6

We shall initially start by trying out the new 6/8 strumming technique with a familiar chord, after which we shall attempt the following chord sequence:

| C | Am | Dm | G |.

Our next song, "House of the rising sun" is written in 6/8 time and will expand our repertoire once more.

House of the rising sun

$\frac{6}{8}$ |Am| C | D | F |Am| C | E | E^7 |

|Am| C | D | F |Am| E |Am| E^7 |

TWO MAIN BARRE TYPES

THE E TYPE

If we take a look at the position for the F chord we see that it is nothing more than the E position with a change in fingers used and one fret across. The index finger has taken over the function of the nut. This barre chord position (the E type) enables us to move along the neck of the guitar and hold down a new chord at each fret. Each chord is one half note higher than the last. If the barre finger is placed in the first fret, then one hears F major. If it is placed in the second fret then one plays F sharp major (or G flat major), in the third fret G major etc.

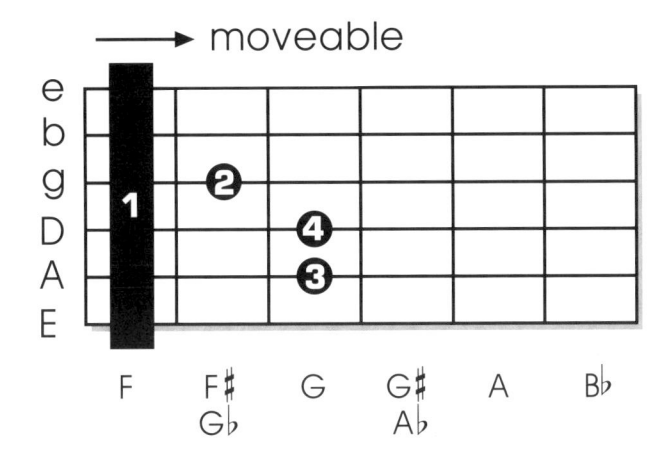

→ moveable

F   F#   G   G#   A   Bb
    Gb   Ab

Logically, the F minor chord (in short Fm) looks like a displaced Em.

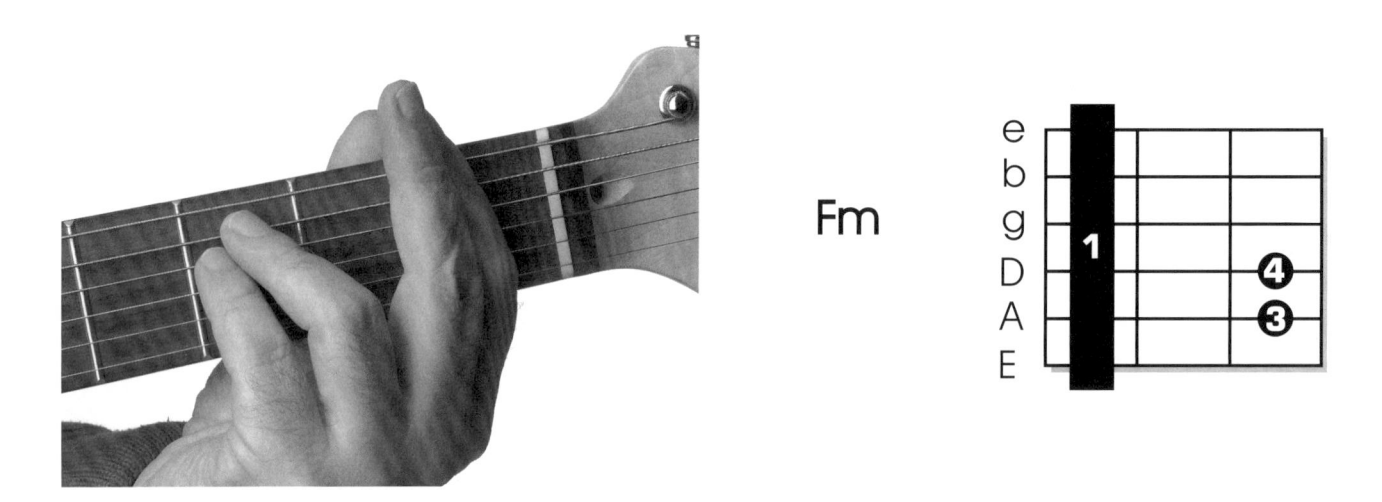

Fm

Likewise, the F^7 chord is created from the position adopted for E^7.

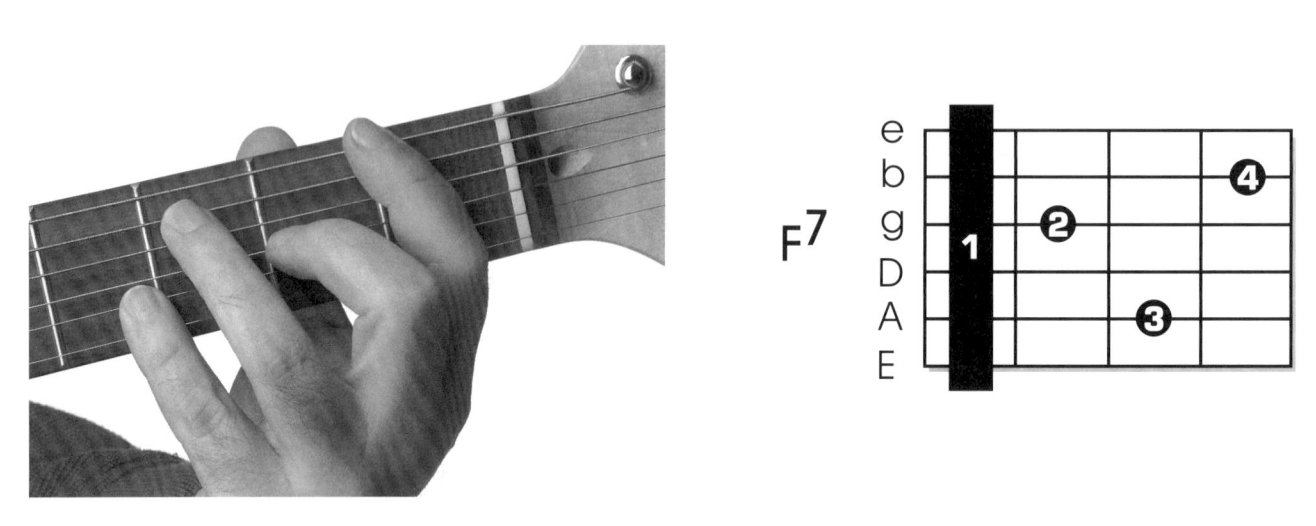

F^7

THE A TYPE

As the name suggests, the A type barre position looks just like a displaced A chord. If the index finger is placed in the 1st fret then we are able to hold down B♭ major (in short B♭).

B♭

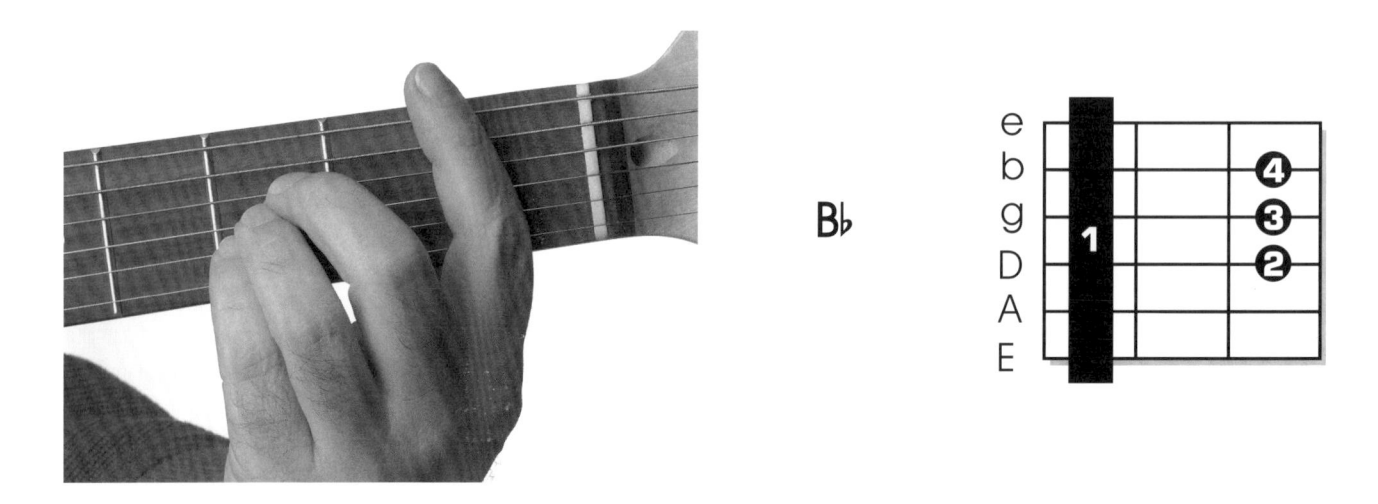

Part 1

In the same way, the B♭ minor (in short B♭m) position is just like that for Am.k.

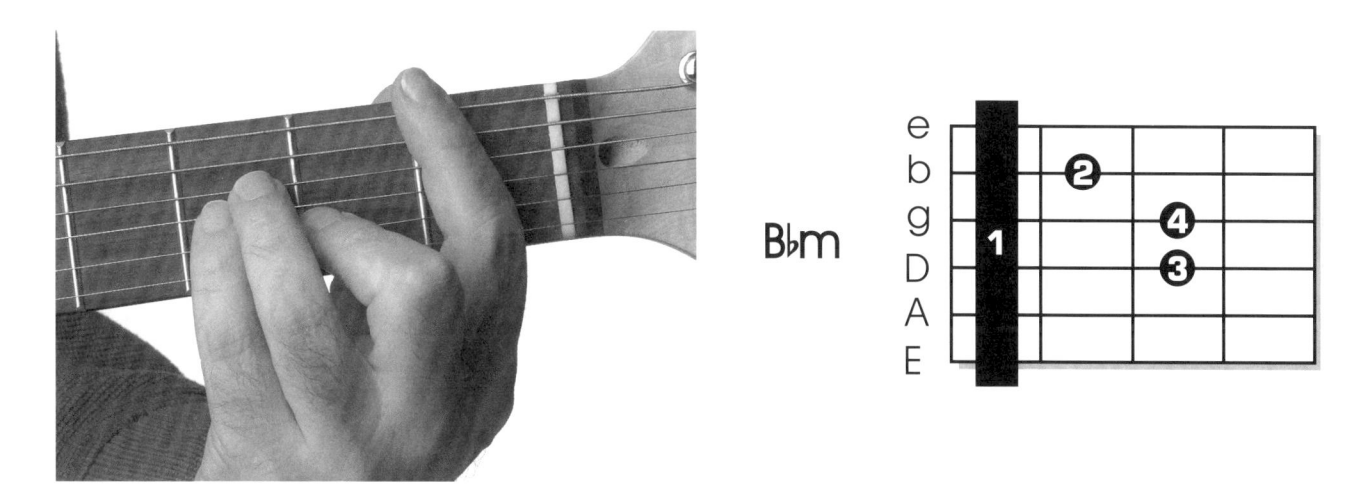

B♭m

The B♭7 chord has a somewhat different appearance to the A7 that we know.

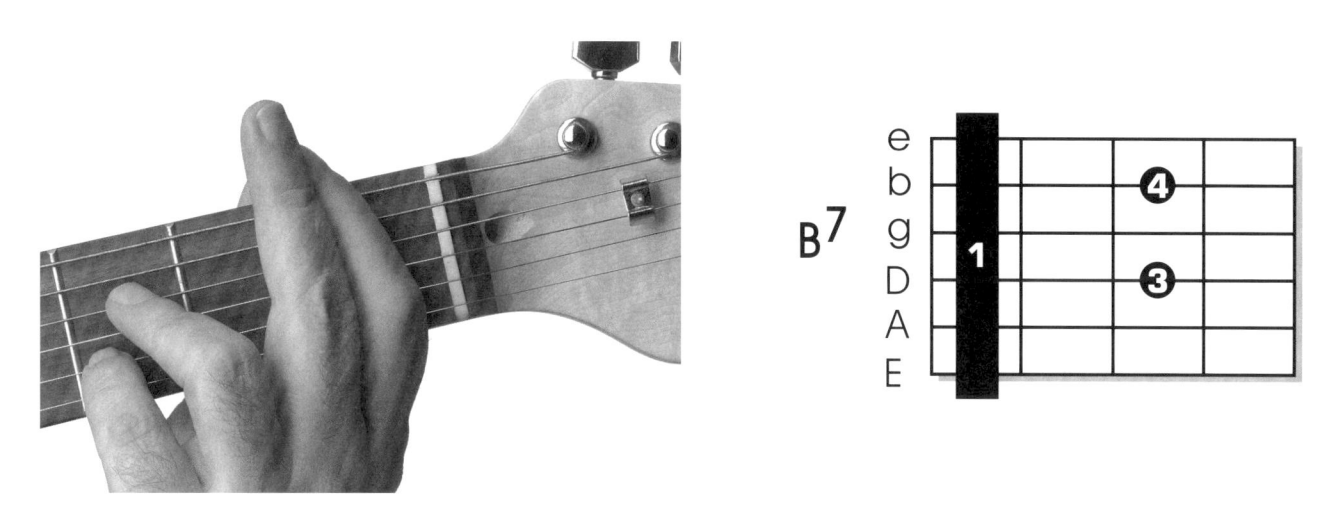

B7

The results of moving the E type barre position along the guitar neck are equally applicable for the A type. Each new fret provides us with a different chord.

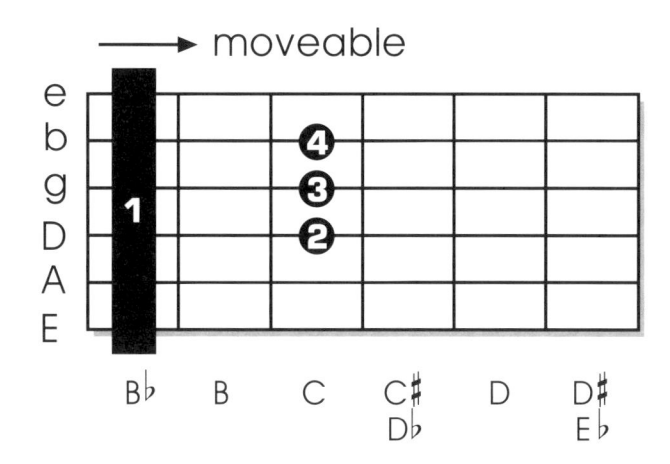

→ moveable

B♭   B   C   C♯/D♭   D   D♯/E♭

25

THE POWERCHORD

The name **powerchord** is used to describe the combination of the first and the fifth note of the scale, in other words the root and fifth notes together (see music theory). The third note, which determines the mode (major or minor), is omitted. The definition of the mode therefore remains intentionally open. In the next two songs, the root is located on the thinner of the two strings played. The fifth lies on the thicker string and therefore sounds a fourth lower than the basic note. The chord diagram shows this clearly:

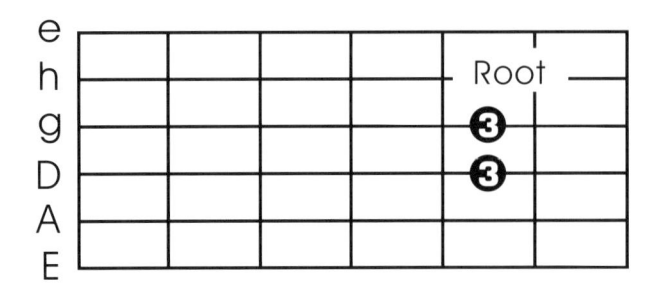

If the root should lie on the thicker of the two strings and therefore sound deeper than the fifth then one usually holds the strings down as shown:

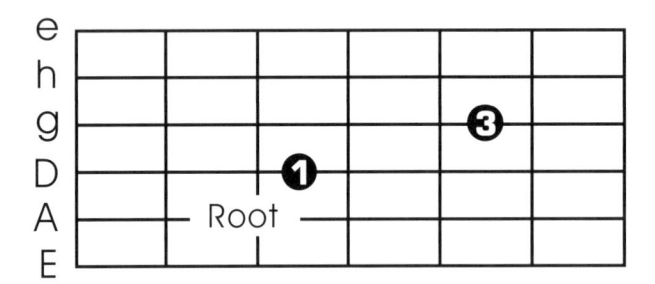

THE COMBINATION OF POWERCHORDS AND HARMONIES
THE FIRE IN YOUR EYES

In the song "The fire in your eyes" we come across a combination of power chords and chord holds.
The riff in this song is played in 4/4 time for a duration of 4 bars.
We play it on the D and G strings in the same fret. We select a stronger distortion with our effect pedals or amplifier and also use a compressor where possible.

The empty strings are each identified with an "0" in the following rhythm diagram.

```
Fret  0 - 0 - 3 - 0  5 | 5 5 - 3 7 → 5 → | 0 - 0 - 5 3 - 0 | 0 ——→
      1 + 2 + 3 + 4 +  | 1 + 2 + 3 + 4 + | 1 + 2 + 3 + 4 + | 1+2+3+4+
```

During the song the riff and chords alternate.

Riff / Riff / Riff / Riff

| B♭ | B♭ |Gm|Gm| E♭ | E♭ | D | D |

| B♭ | B♭ |Gm|Gm| E♭ | E♭ | D | D | G | G |

Riff / Riff

THE RIFF FROM THE SONG „MAKE ME MOVE"

The song "Make Me Move" centres around a two bar riff in 4/4 time. Here is the schematic diagram:

Fret   5 → 5 → 0 3 | 5 — 5 — 8 7 →
           1 + 2 + 3 + 4 + | 1 + 2 + 3 + 4 +

The riffs and chords also alternate in this song.

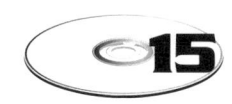

Riff / Riff / Riff / Riff

| A♭ | E♭ |Cm| G |

| A♭ | E♭ |Cm| G |

Riff / Riff / Riff / Riff

PLAYING SINGLE NOTES

POSITIONING YOUR HANDS

We shall use the same numbers for the fingers as before:

Index finger	=	1
Middle finger	=	2
Ring finger	=	3
Little finger	=	4

As previously explained, the digit "0" appears when an empty string is to be strummed. The thumb, which is always placed on the rear of the guitar neck, is not given a number.

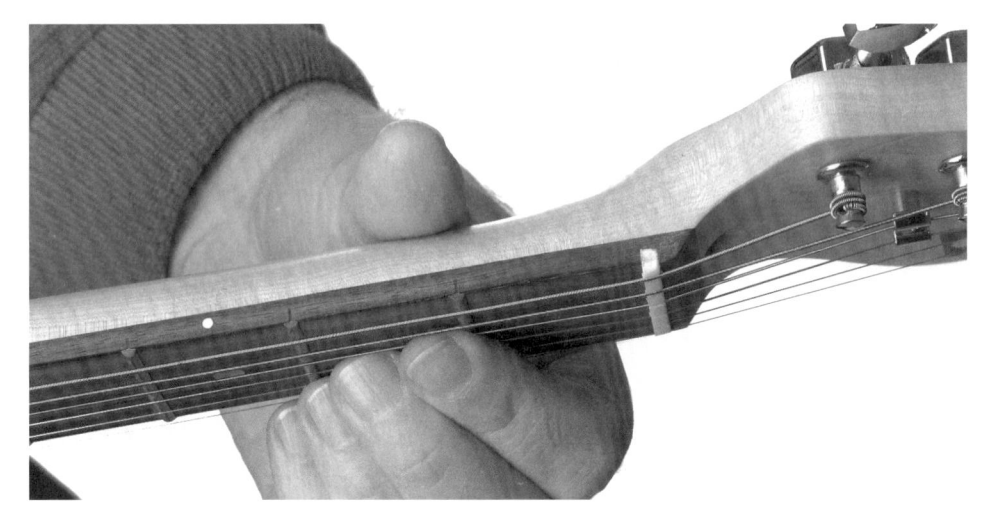

To identify the finger on the right hand we use the abbreviations of their spanish names:

Thumb	=	p (pulgar)
Index finger	=	i (indice)
Middle finger	=	m (media)
Ring finger	=	a (anular)

The little finger, which has no function here, is held in a relaxed position against the other fingers and never stretched out.

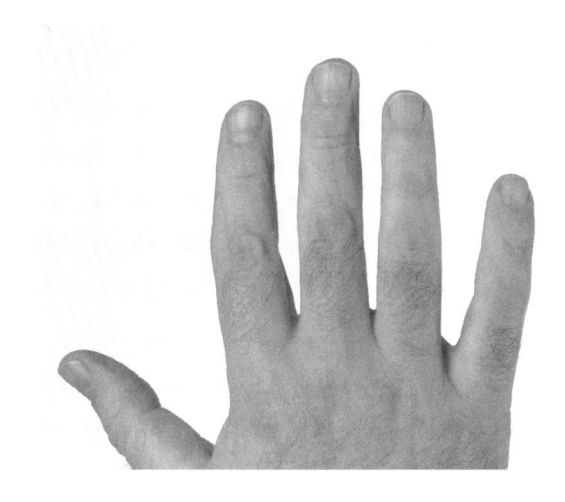

PICKING TECHNIQUE

Place your thumb on one of the bottom three strings and stretch it out so that the tip extends towards the next string up. Now slide it down and across the string, passing the adjacent string without moving it. This stroking technique is known as **free stroking** and is also referred to using the Spanish word **tirando**.

The index, middle and ring fingers stroke the strings in the direction of the next deepest string. Each stroking finger presses lightly on its string, pushing it gently towards the ceiling. In contrast to tirando, **apoyando** comprises of resting strokes, in which the fingers are placed upon the adjacent strings **after each stroke**.

THE OPEN STRINGS

In order to learn how to play using single notes we first require some theoretical knowledge. It is therefore essential to work through the next chapter in this book "music notation", in the music theory section. Just as we need to recognise letters in order to read words and sentences, so too we require a basic understanding of the "building blocks" of music, in order to be able to create music.

A good knowledge of the names of the notes, their values and distribution within bars is an absolute must if one is to work with music successfully.

Before we come to playing notes, we should first practise stroking the empty strings for exercise.

We shall allocate the strings to our fingers as follows:

    e string = Ring finger (a)
    b string = Middle finger (m)
    g string = Index finger (i)

The thumb is responsible for the D, A and E strings.
The notes produced by the empty strings appear in music notation as follows:

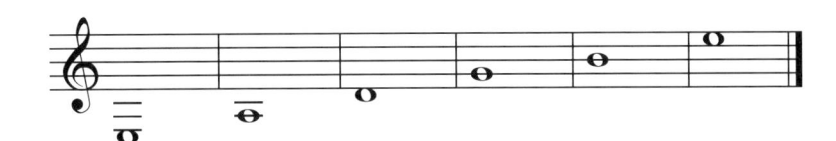

Strike the empty strings a number of times, in order to gain a feel for the production of a note.

Now we shall play the following practise pieces:

16

17

18

Work slowly through the exercises initially, counting out loud as you play.
Only once you are able to play through the sequences of notes fluidly should you attempt to increase the tempo. We shall use this method for all subsequent exercises and songs.

THE NOTES ON THE G STRING

Notation:

g (open)   a

The note "a" is produced by placing the 2nd finger on the g string in the 2nd fret. The string is stroked by the index finger on the right hand (i).

Exercise:

THE NOTES ON THE B STRING

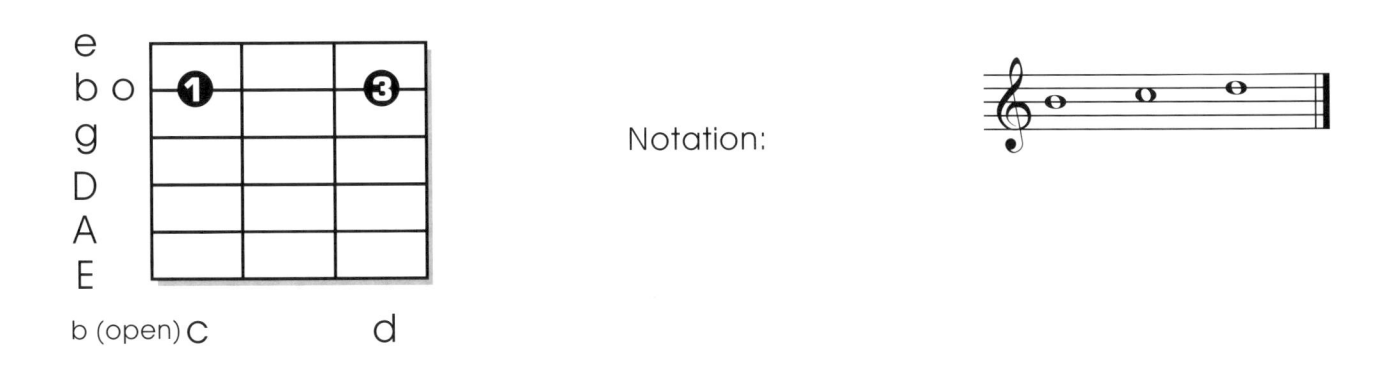

Notation:

b (open) C   d

The note "c" is produced by placing the 1st finger on the b string in the 1st fret. The string is stroked by the middle finger on the right hand (m)

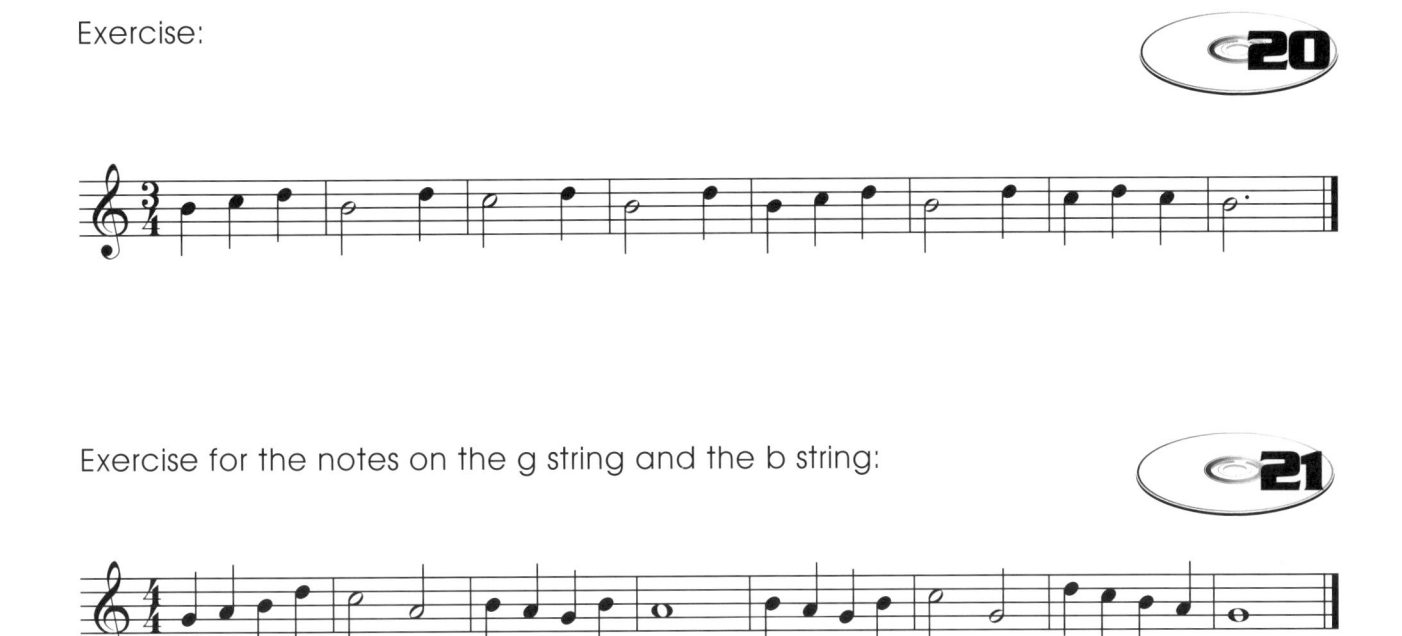

Exercise:

Exercise for the notes on the g string and the b string:

SONG:
OH, WHEN THE SAINTS

We can now play our first song using single notes:
"Oh, when the saints".

Oh, when the saints

THE NOTES ON THE E STRING

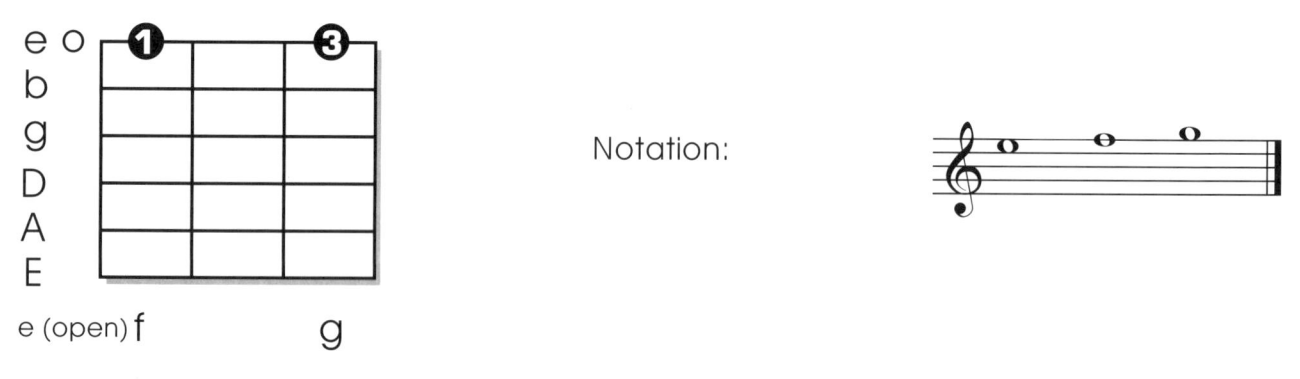

e (open)   f   g

Notation:

The note "f" is produced by placing the 1st finger on the e string in the 1st fret. The note "g" is produced by placing the 3rd finger in the 3rd fret. The string is stroked by the ring finger of the right hand (a).

Exercise:

Exercise for the notes on the g, b and e strings:

Now we shall use the notes that we've learned to play the cowboy song "Down in the valley".

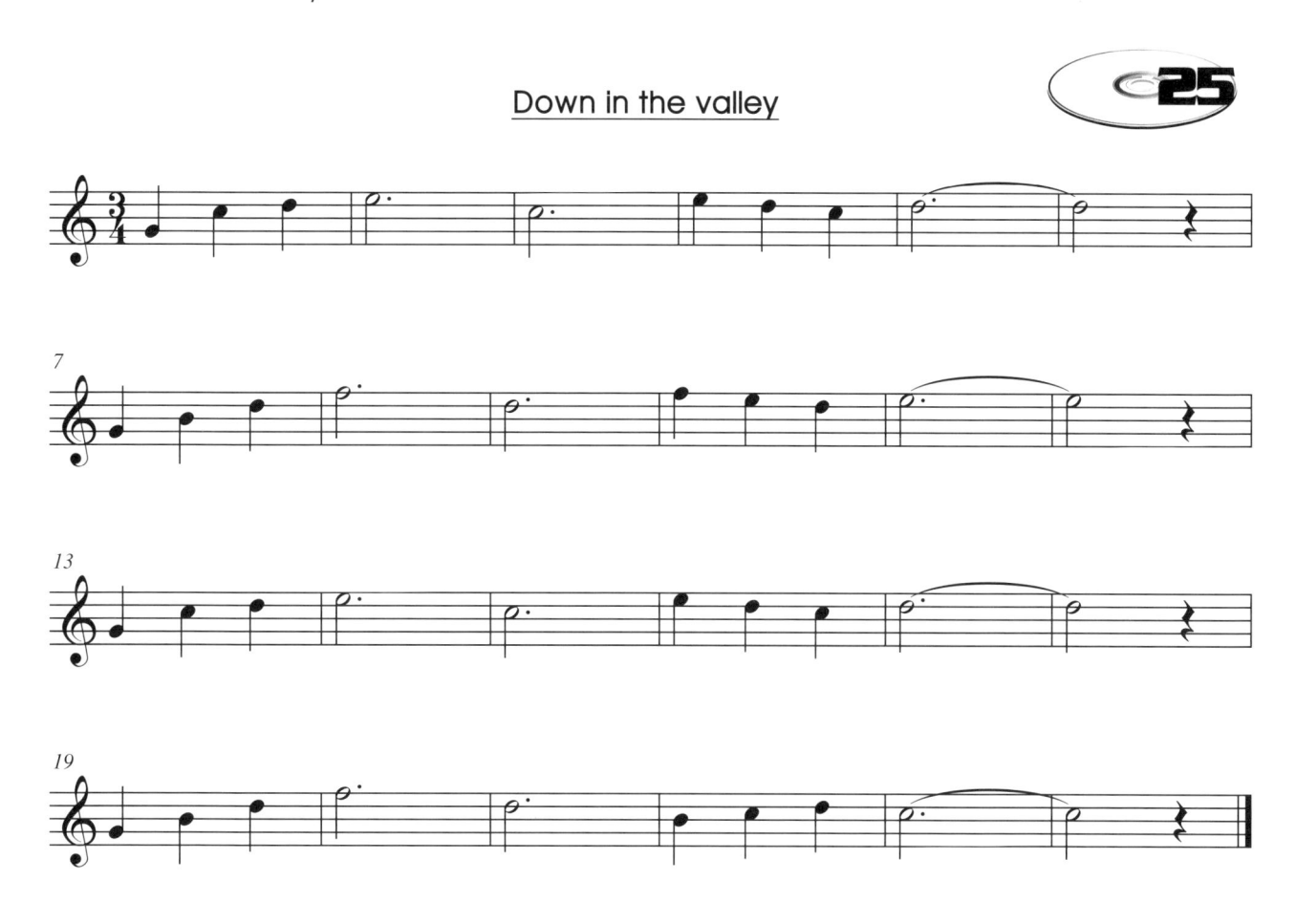

Down in the valley

THE NOTES ON THE D STRING

Notation:

D (open)   e   f

The note "e" is produced by placing the 2nd finger on the D string in the 2nd fret. The note "f" is produced by placing the 3rd finger in the 3rd fret. The string is stroked using the thumb.

Exercise:

THE NOTES ON THE A STRING

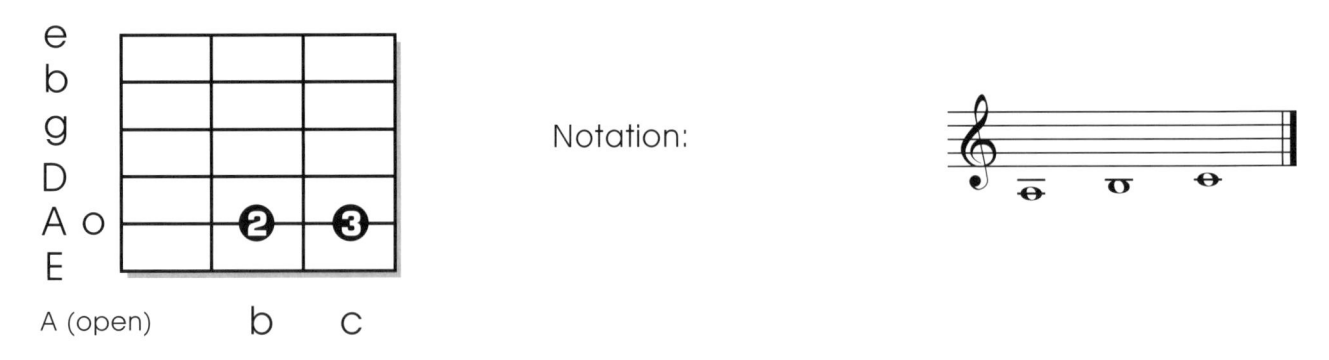

Notation:

A (open) b c

The note "b" is produced by placing the 2nd finger on the A string in the 2nd fret. The note "c" is produced by placing the 3rd finger in the 3rd fret. The string is stroked using the thumb.
Exercise:

Exercise for the notes on the D and A strings:

The song "I can't believe it" can be played using the notes on the D and A strings.

I can't believe it

THE NOTES ON THE E STRING

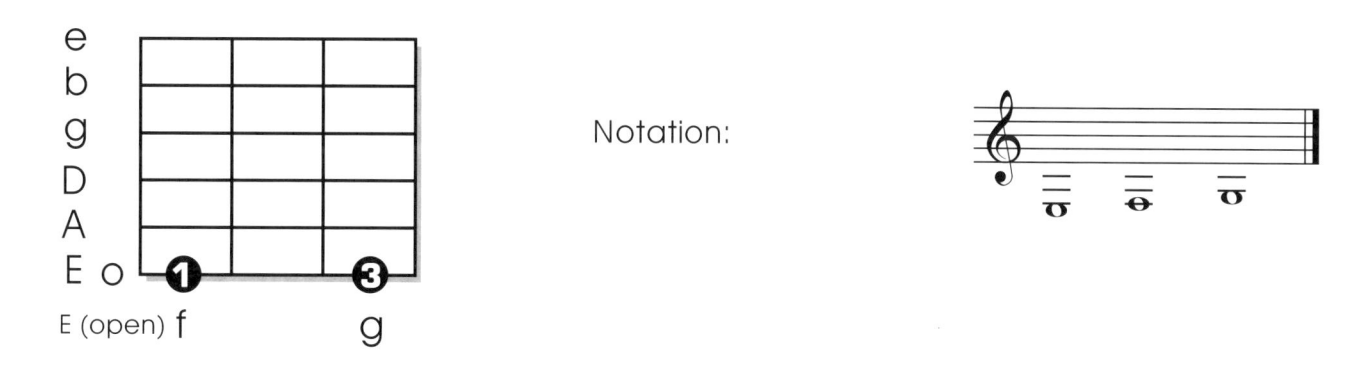

Notation:

E (open) f   g

The note "f" is produced by placing the 1st finger on the E string in the 1st fret. The note "g" is produced by placing the 3rd finger in the 3rd fret. The string is stroked using the thumb.

Exercise:

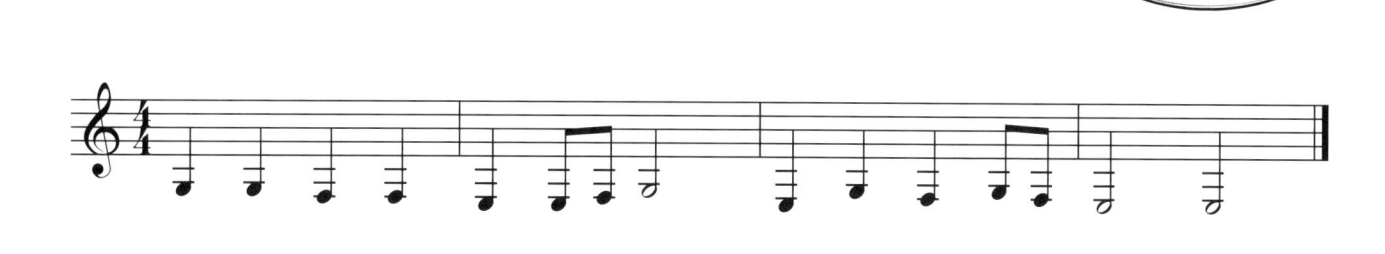

Exercise for the notes on the D, A and E strings:

We shall use the notes from the three lowest strings to play 2 songs:
"Tom Dooley" and "John Brown's body".

Tom Dooley

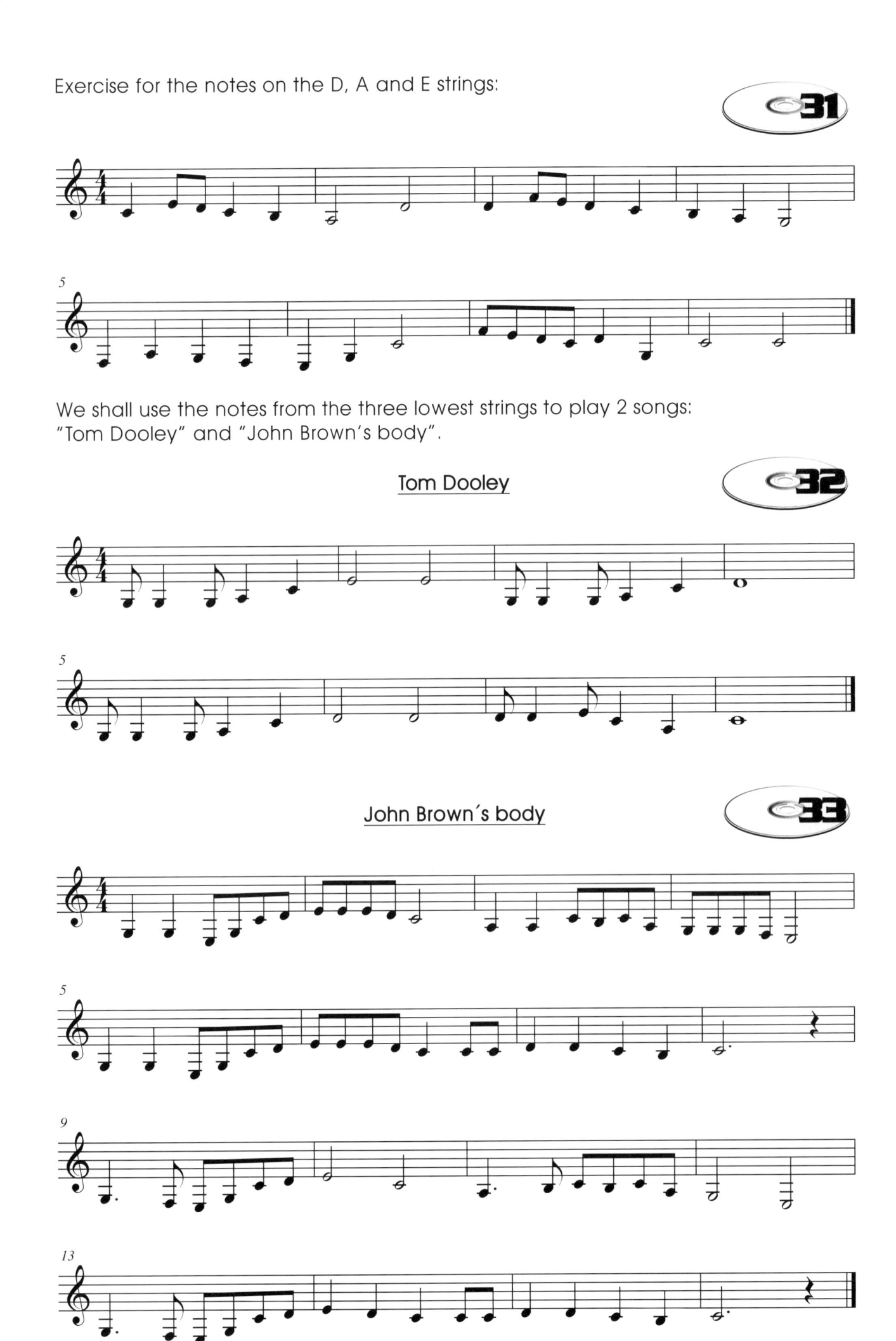

John Brown's body

THE NOTES WITH ♯ AND ♭

Up to now we have only worked with the seven root notes. Now we also want to get to know the notes in the frets with which we are not yet familiar, those which we have not yet used on each of the strings.

These notes each have two names. For example the note that we produce on the 3rd fret on the g string is known both as A sharp and as B flat. The names of the new notes are created using the name of the root note in the direction from which they originate. If the direction of origin is the root note a, then A♯ is created. However, if the root note of origin is B then B♭ is created. The interchanging of note names is called "enharmonic exchange" (see music theory).

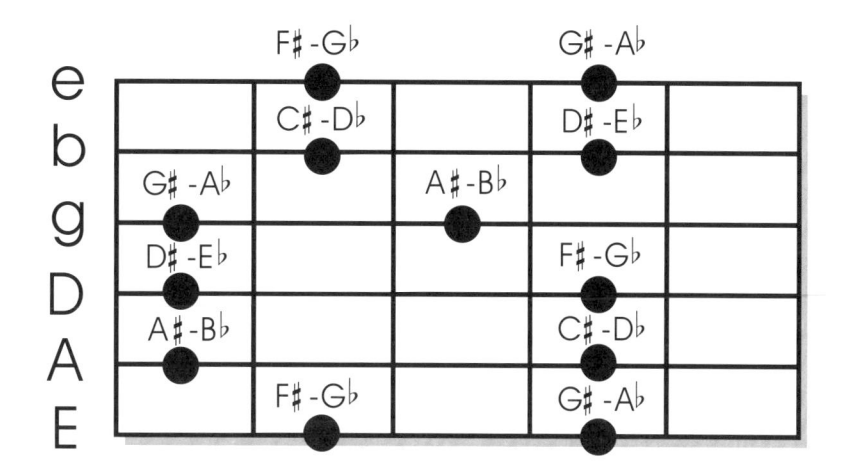

TABLATURE NOTATION

In addition to note-based music notation, a numbers and symbols system also exists and is most commonly used in American publications. It is known as tablature. Six lines are used to depict the guitar strings and these are scattered with numbers which denote the frets in which each string is to be held.

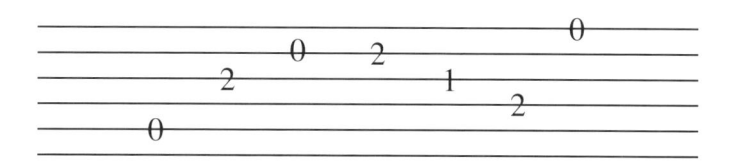

0In contrast to the chord diagrams already familiar to us, these numbers do not refer to the fingers on the left hand but instead to the frets. The schematic layout of the string positions is however the same.

If multiple numbers appear over one another then these sounds are to be played at the same time. An "0" denotes an empty string.

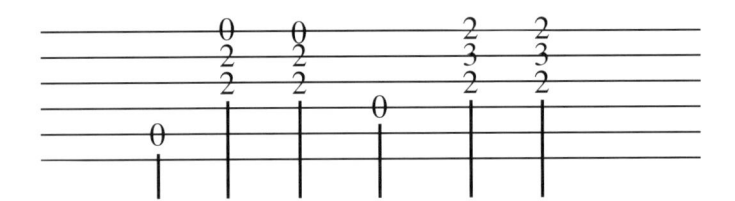

The lengths of the sounds are shown using symbols, the appearances of which very closely reflect those used in notation; the pause symbols are exactly the same as those used in notation. Here is a comparison between notes and tablature:

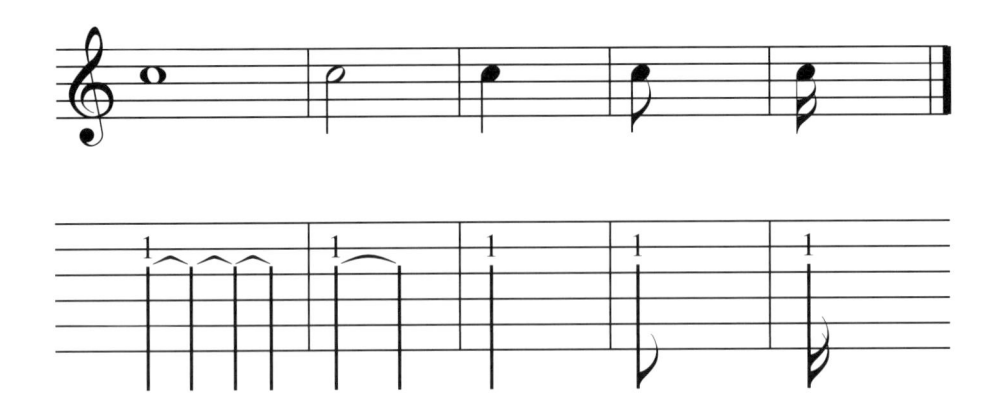

Combinations of multiple quavers and semi-quavers are also possible.

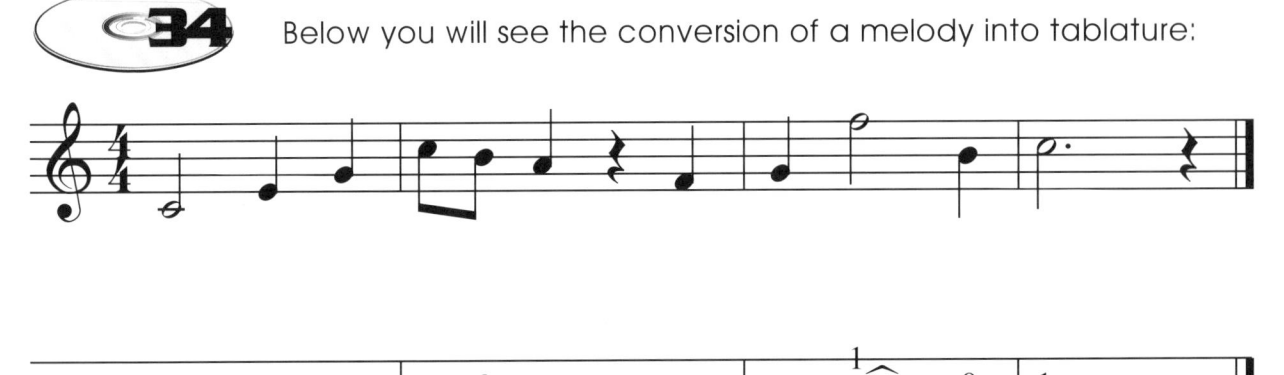

Below you will see the conversion of a melody into tablature:

ACCOMPANYING SONGS WITH CHORDS

In addition to strumming using a plectrum (across all strings), there is a range of options for strumming using the fingers of the picking hand.

Initially, we need to look at simultaneous strumming using the index, middle and ring fingers (i-m-a), which we use in alternation with strumming using the thumb. We also hold down the D major chord with the left hand and strum in alternation with the A string (thumb) and the three strings g-h-e (using i-m-a).

The arrangement of the notes appears as follows:

The following strumming technique is usually used in order to accompany a song in 3/4 time:

One can accompany songs in 4/4 time using a combination of strumming variations. The techniques most often used are depicted in the arrangement below.

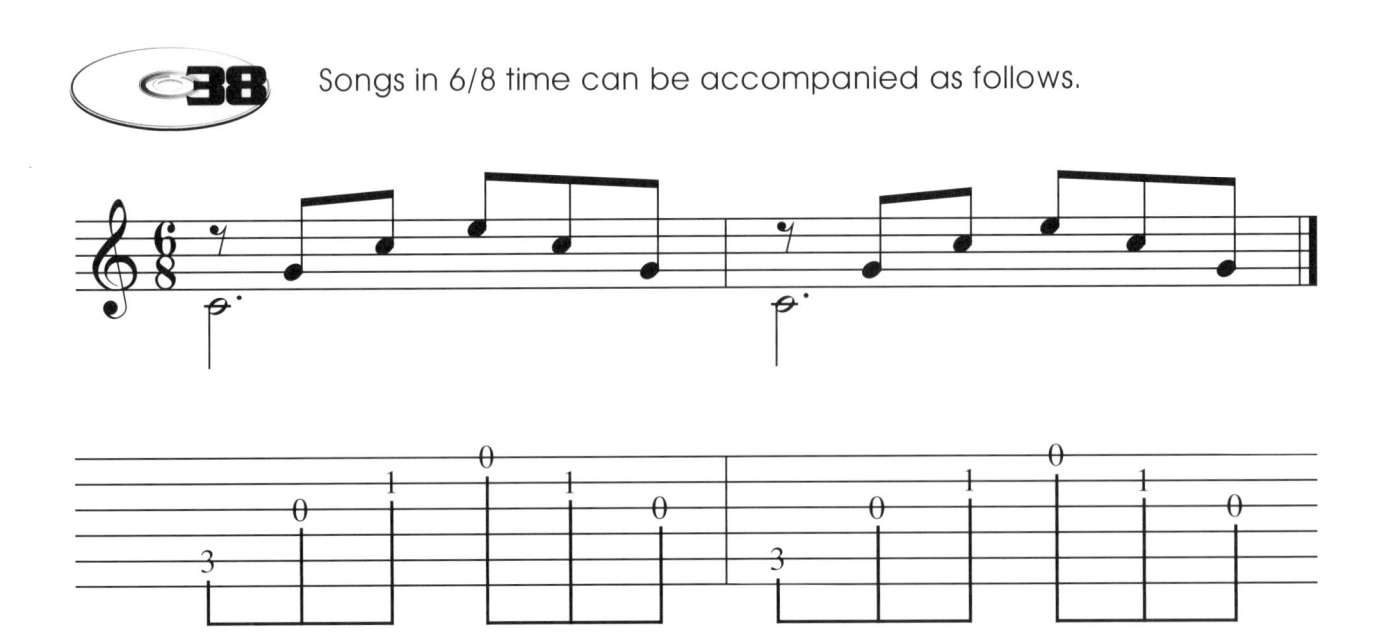

37

38 Songs in 6/8 time can be accompanied as follows.

Part 3

MUSICAL NOTATION

THE STAVES

Just as we use the letters of the alphabet to write down our language, so too we use notes to write down pieces of music.
To do so we require **staves**, which comprise of 5 lines and 4 spaces. These are counted from the bottom upward.

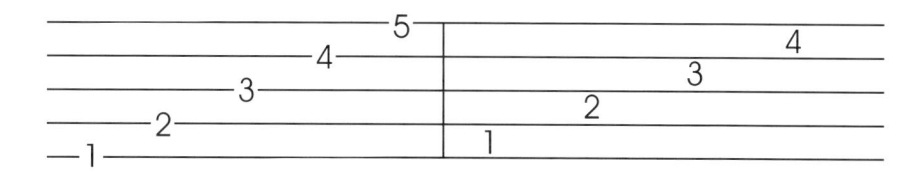

The placement of notes on a staff provides information on the pitch of a note. The higher the note on the staff, the higher the sound of the note.

THE NAMES OF THE NOTES

We use seven root notes, the names of which are taken from letters of the alphabet.

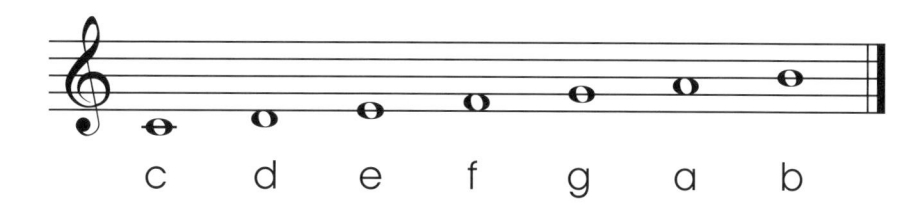

c   d   e   f   g   a   b

The 7 root notes always recur in the same sequence in the higher and lower ranges. In order to write down notes which lie above or below the 5 lines of the staff, one draws so-called **leger lines**, which occur at the same distances as the lines on the staff.

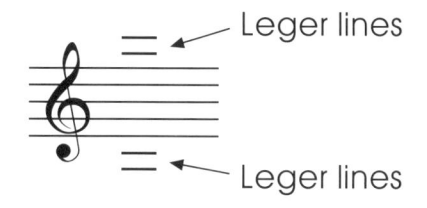

Leger lines

Leger lines

THE CLEF

In order to be able to specifically define the notes drawn on the staves, we use a **clef**. Guitar music is written down with the aid of the violin clef, also known as the G-clef. The 2nd line of the staff is encircled by the curl of the clef, showing that the note "g" should lie on this line.
If a small "8" is drawn at the base of the clef, this shows that the notes played should all be played an octave deeper than shown. This is standard when playing guitar.

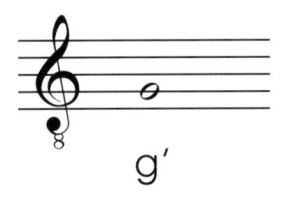

g'

THE OCTAVES

The distance between one note and the next note with the same name is known as an **octave**. In order to be able to clearly define the same note in a different range each of the octaves is given a different name.

The central starting point is "middle C". This note is so-called because it lies right in the centre of a piano keyboard. This is where the so-called "**one line octave**" begins, the notes in which are followed by a stroke (c'). Following this comes the "**two line octave**", the "**three line octave**" etc.

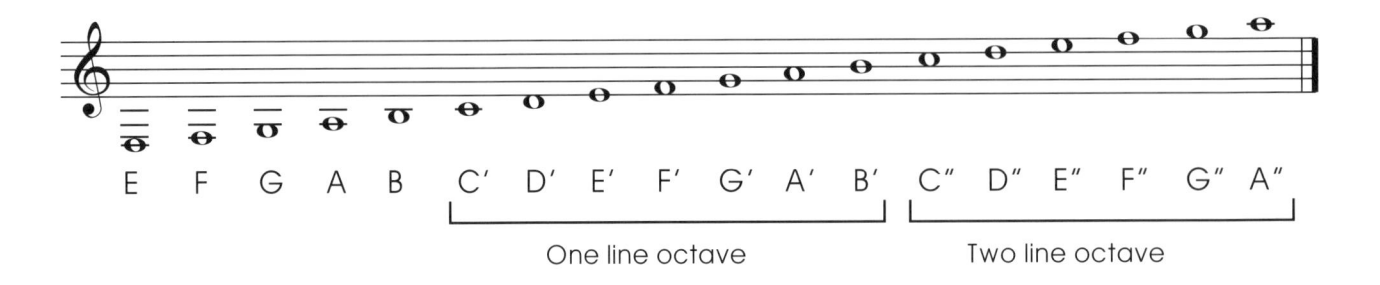

E   F   G   A   B   C' D' E' F' G' A' B'   C" D" E" F" G" A"
                    |_____One line octave_____| |_____Two line octave_____|

Part 3

THE NOTE VALUES

In order to understand something of the length or duration of the notes, we must look at their **appearance**.

A **whole note (Semibreve)** is drawn as a circle and has a value (length) of 4 so-called **beats**.

It can be divided into two **half notes (minims)** which are shown as note heads (circles) with note stems, each of which has a value of **2 beats**.

The **half note** can once again be divided in two, leaving two **quarter notes (crotchets)** which are drawn as filled-in note heads, each with a value of **one beat**. The crotchet forms the basis for counting a bar.

The depiction of further subdivisions is possible through the addition of flags to the note stems:
Eighth note (quaver)   =   one flag,
Sixteenth note (semi-quaver) =   two flags etc.

If a number of notes with flags are drawn in sequence then they can be connected together using note beams. From the third staff line upwards the note stem is drawn on the left pointing downwards, whilst below this line the stem is drawn on the right pointing upwards.
Below is an overview of the most important note values:

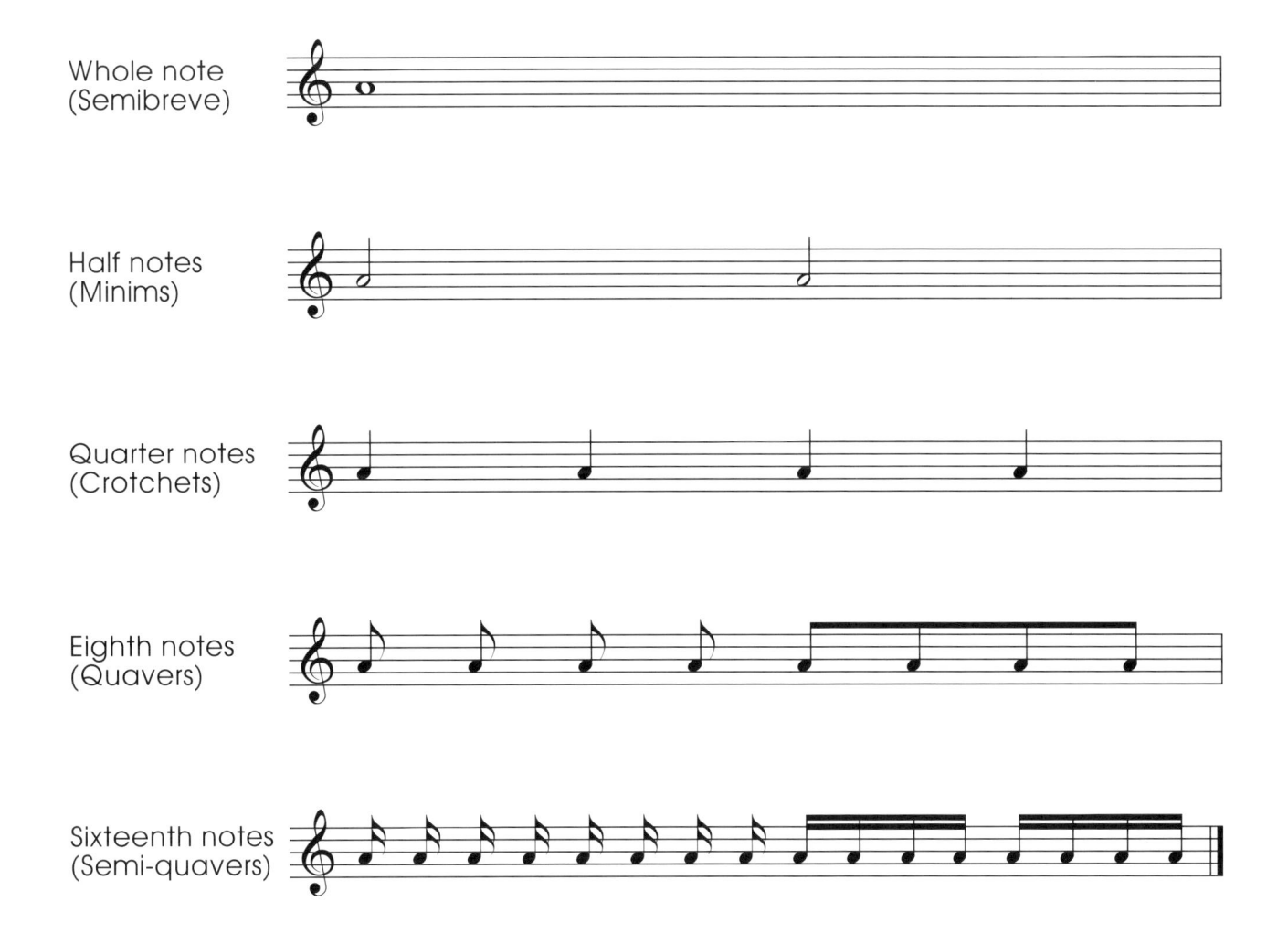

Whole note (Semibreve)

Half notes (Minims)

Quarter notes (Crotchets)

Eighth notes (Quavers)

Sixteenth notes (Semi-quavers)

43

THE DOT AND THE TIE

The **dot** behind a note extends its original value by one half. If for example, a dot follows a minim, then the one additional beat is added to its standard two beat value. This **dotted minim** now has a value of **three beats**.
This process can be applied to all note values.

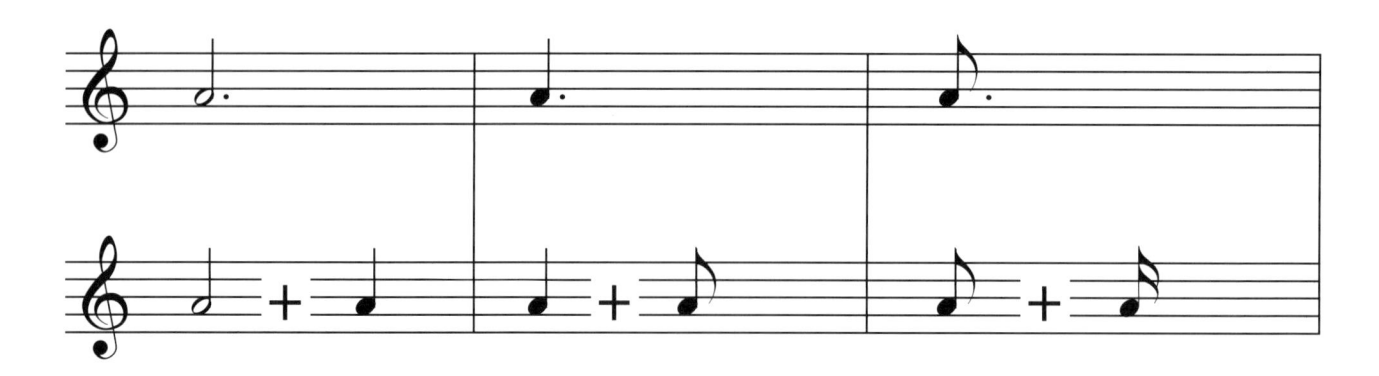

A further method of extending the value of a note is to add a **tie**, which joins together two notes of the same pitch. This also permits the length of a note to exceed the bar in which it is placed.

THE RESTS

The values of the reste are equal to the note values:

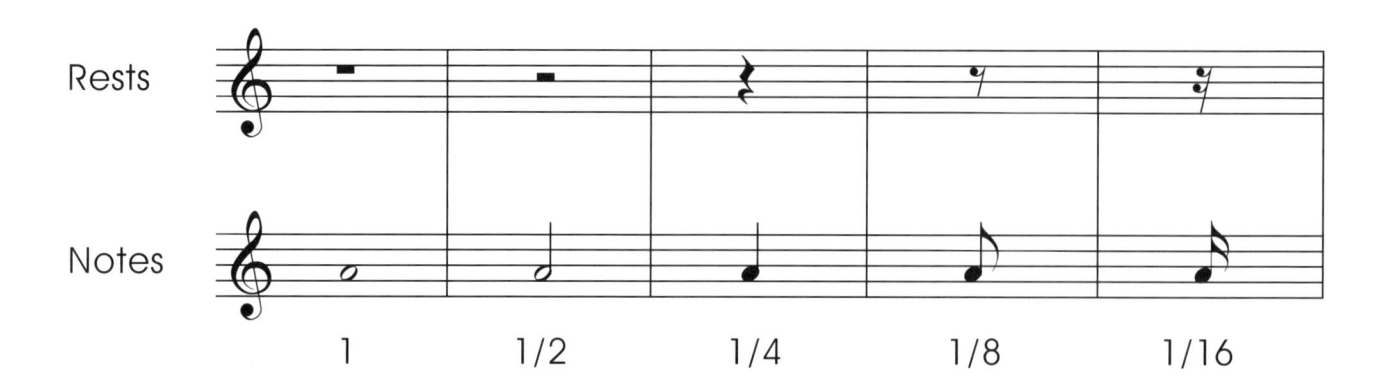

Rests					
Notes	1	1/2	1/4	1/8	1/16

THE TRIPLET

An alternative to halving a note value when subdividing it, is to divide it into three: Creating a triplet. For example, three crotchets (quarter notes) can be played as crotchet triplets in the time of a minim (half note), or three quavers can be played as quaver triplets in the time of a crotchet etc.

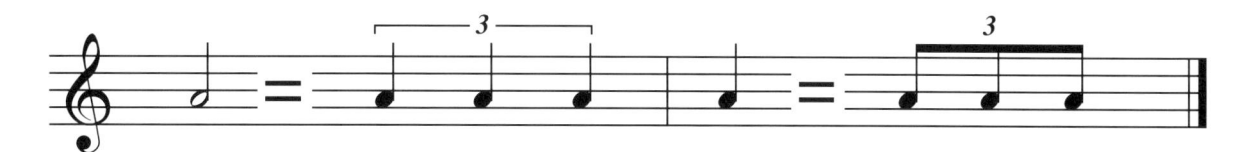

THE ACCIDENTALS

If a hash symbol (♯) stands before a note then it is raised by one semitone.

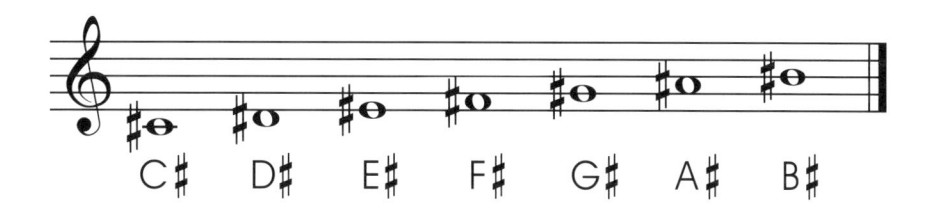

Internationally the "♯" ign is attached after the note name, e.g. C♯, D♯ etc.
If a B (♭) is placed behind a note then the note is lowered by one semitone.
Internationally the "♭" sign is attached after the note name, e.g. C♭, D♭ etc.

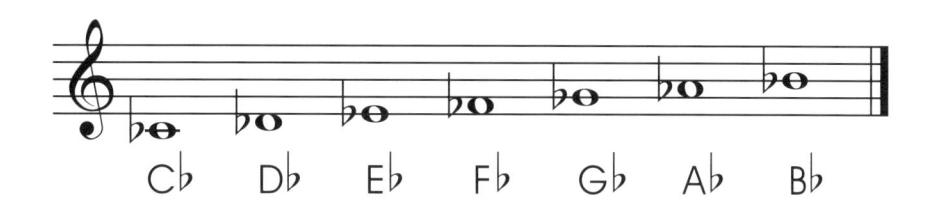

The accidentals apply for the duration of a bar and are lifted at the start of the next bar. An additional method of lifting the accidental within a bar is with the addition of a "natural" symbol (♮), the effect of which is limited to the bar in which it appears.

If accidentals are to be valid throughout the entire piece of music then they are placed at the beginning of the piece and are then known as the **key signature**.
The raising or lowering of each tone then applies to all octaves.

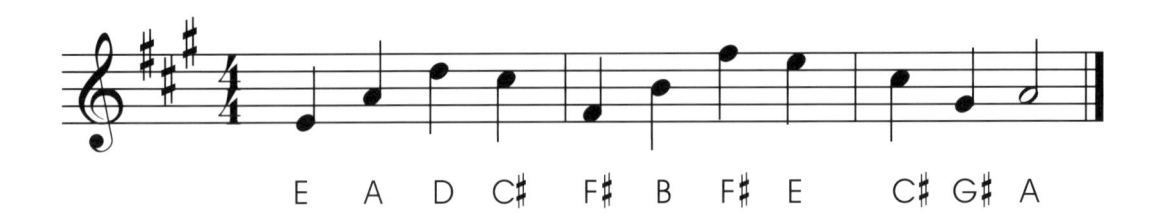

BARS

A piece of music is divided into equal sections by lines known as **bar lines**. In addition to the single bar line, larger sections may also be separated by **double bar lines**, whilst the **final double bar** indicates the end of the piece.

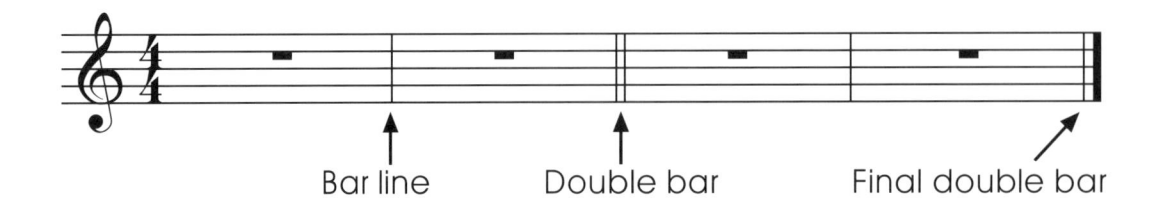

Bar line　　Double bar　　Final double bar

After the signature key comes a fraction known as the **time signature**. The bottom number indicates the note value, whilst the top number shows how many beats are in each bar.

The first note after the bar line is accented. If two unaccented beats follow then we call this **ternary time**.
If one unaccented beat follows then we call this **binary time**. In both cases we differentiate between **simple time**, which comprises of 2 or 3 counting units and **compound time**, which has 4 or more.

Examples of simple time signatures: 2/4, 3/4, 3/8
Examples of compound time signatures: 4/4 (= c), 6/8, 9/8

If one counts minims in place of crotchets in 4/4 time then one uses the symbol ¢, known as **alla breve**.

THE ANACRUSIS (UPBEAT)

An incomplete bar at the beginning of a piece is known as the **anacrusis**.
When added together with an incomplete bar at the end of a piece, the anacrusis forms one complete bar.

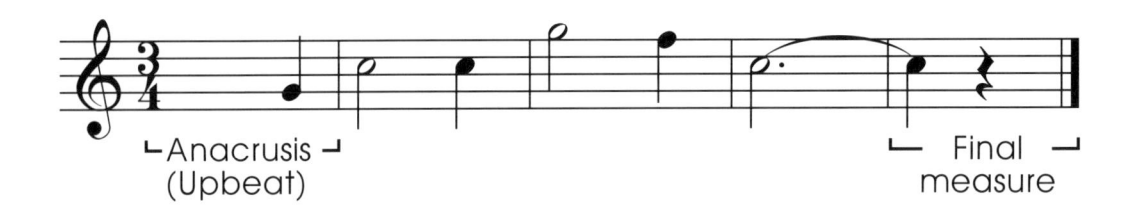

└ Anacrusis ┘
(Upbeat)

└ Final ┘
measure

SYNCOPATION

Syncopation occurs when an accent is placed on a usually anaccented beat in a bar. The previously accented beat in the bar remains without accent or is omitted by way of a tie or a pause.

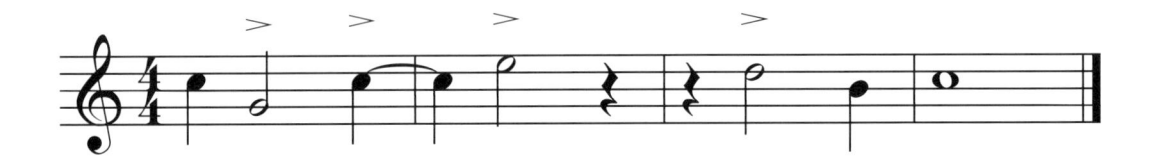

THE REPEAT SIGN

The two dots are the start and end of a section of music are known as repeat signs. They indicate that the section in between should be played on more time.

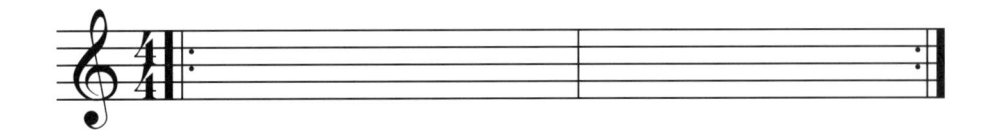

If, following the repeat, a different ending should be played then this is shown with **brackets**.

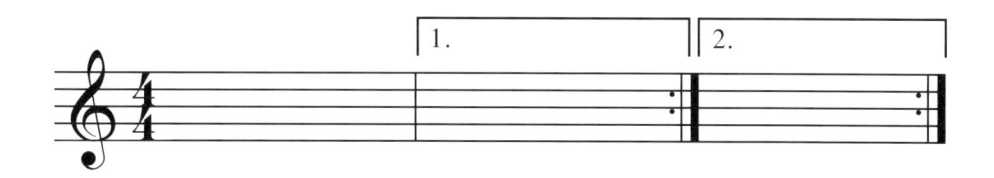

D. C. al fine means:	from the start to the "Fine" (End), without a repeat this time.
⊕ - ⊕	the section between the "coda signs" should be replayed one more time without repeat.
D. S. (Dal Segno)	indicates that the musician should play one more time from this sign.

THE FERMATA

The fermata (⌒) is a hold sign, which may be placed over notes or pauses. It shows that the note or pause beneath it is to be held for a longer duration than is actually indicated by its value.

THE CIRCLE OF FIFTHS

THE MAJOR SCALE

A **scale** is a specific progression of tones in steps across one octave. However the tones do not all have the same distance from one another. We differentiate between **whole steps** and **half steps**. The smallest possible distance between two tones is called a **half step**. **Two** of these **half steps** equal one whole step. The frets on a guitar are arranged in half steps.

If one holds down one tone on a string then the next highest and next lowest tone on this string are each one semitone away. The tone on the next but one fret is a whole tone step higher or lower than the starting tone.

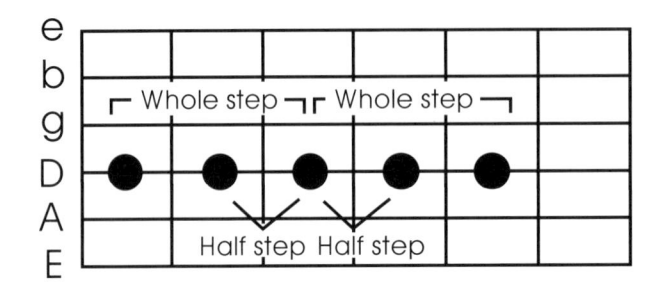

The **major scale** comprises of 8 tones, whereby the last tone lies one octave away from the basic tone, therefore having the same name.
It can be divided into two halves (**tetrachords**), each of which comprises of two whole tone steps and one semitone step.
The half steps are located between the 3rd and 4th tone and again between the 7th and 8th tone as shown:

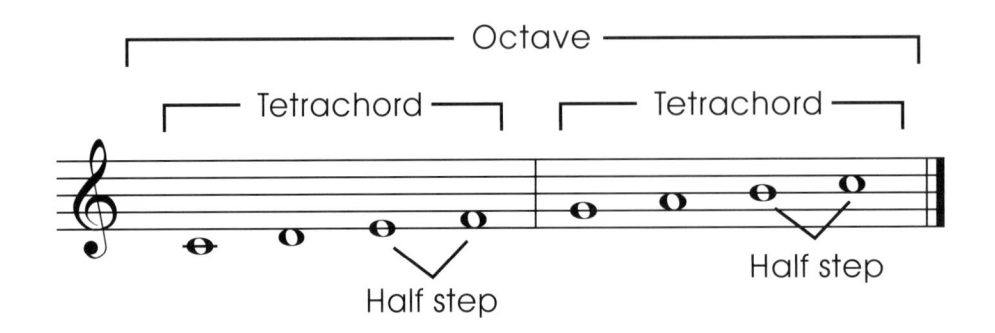

The position of the semitones are particularly visible on the piano keyboard. We shall look at the C major scale here, as this serves as the basis for all subsequent scales.

We are able to create further a scale from the basic tone of the second tetrachord upward. This scale is called the **G major scale** and takes its name from its basic tone. In order to adhere to the basic construction principle of the major scales we must **raise** the seventh tone with the aid of a sharp sign (f becomes f#).

The distance between the basic tone of the first scale, C, and the basic tone of the second scale, G, is known as a "fifth" and the relationship between the two basic tones is called the **fifth-relationship.**

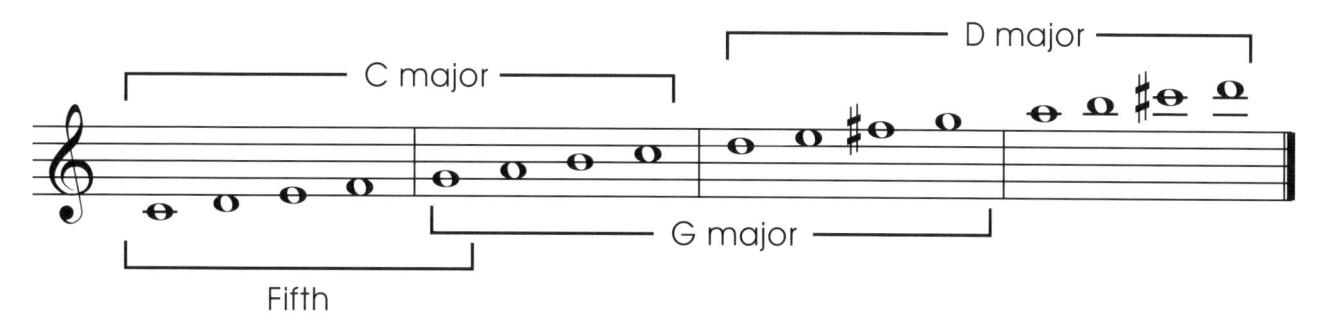

This process can be continued, creating a total of 12 major scales by raising the 7th step each time.

If one views the lower tetrachord from the C major scale as the upper tetrachord of the F major scale, then one can create a whole new set of scales in this direction. When moving down through the scales in this direction we must observe the basic construction principle of the major scales in reverse and lower the 4th tone of the lower tetrachord with the aid of a ♭.

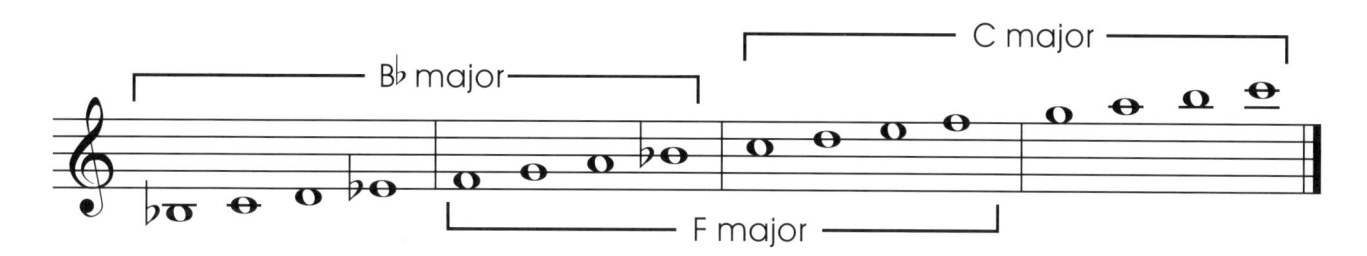

Continuing with this process enables us to create 12 scales, each of which has one more ♭-accidental within it.

In order to avoid any confusion regarding the raising and lowering of tones we need to remember that the 6 keys with sharp signs are the same keys (in terms of sound) as those 6 keys marked with flat signs.

More on this in the next chapter.

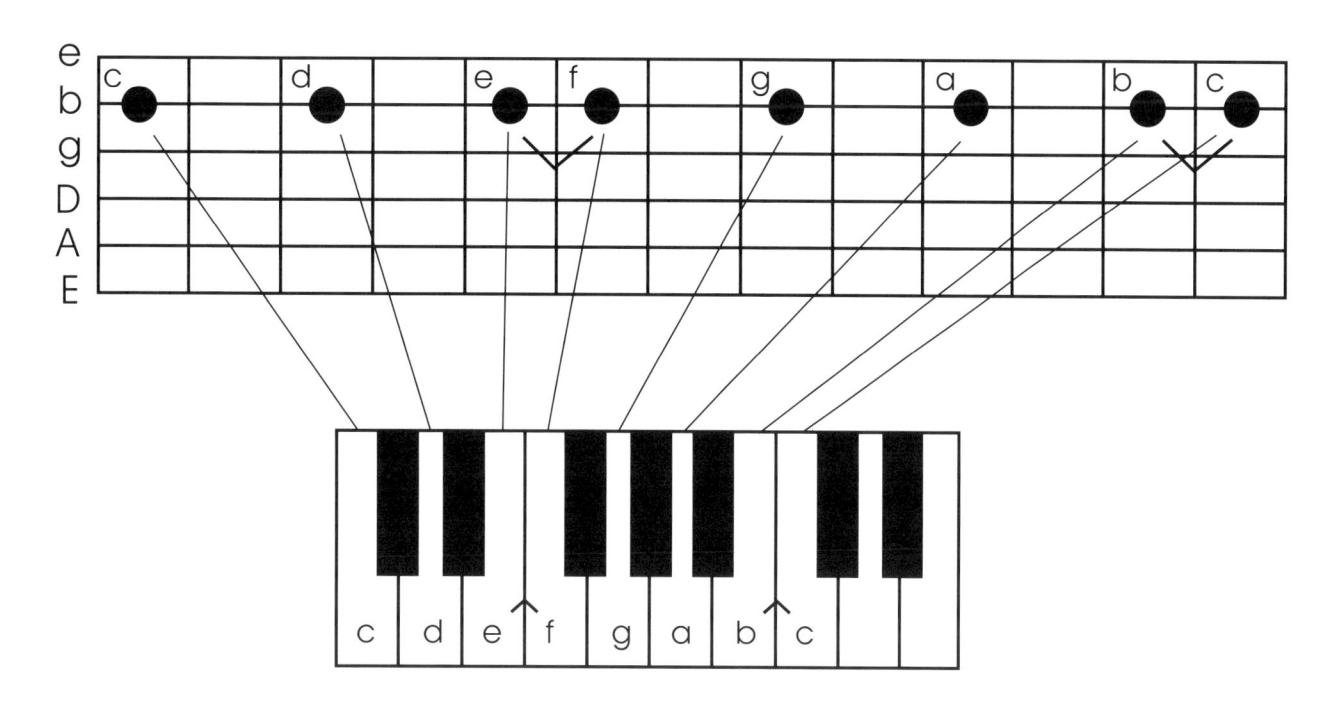

THE MAJOR CIRCLE OF FIFTHS

In order to gain a solid overview one places the keys in a circle. The circle is divided into one half containing the sharps, and one half containing the flats.
These two halves meet in the middle at F♯ major / G♭ major.

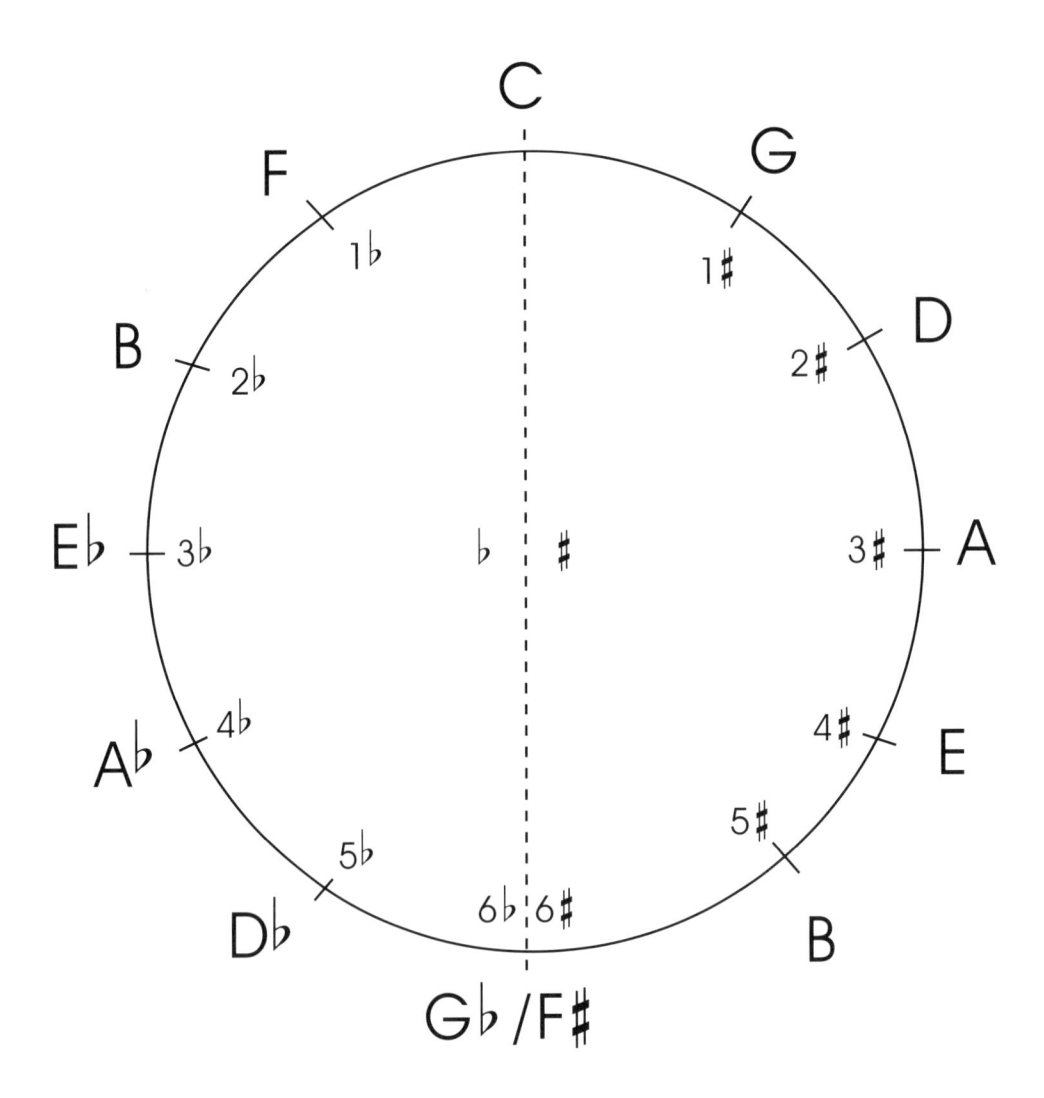

The distance (or **interval**) between one basic tone and the next (in a clockwise direction) is one **fifth**, thus we call this diagram the **circle of fifths**. The circle of fifths contains all of the major scales.

ACCIDENTALS

Every key has its accidentals and the sequence of these sharps and flats is also specified. At the start of written music you will see which notes are to be raised and lowered throughout the piece.
The sequence of the sharps for this purpose runs: F#, C#, G#, D#, A#, E#.
The sequence of the flats runs: B, E♭, A♭, D♭, G♭, C♭.

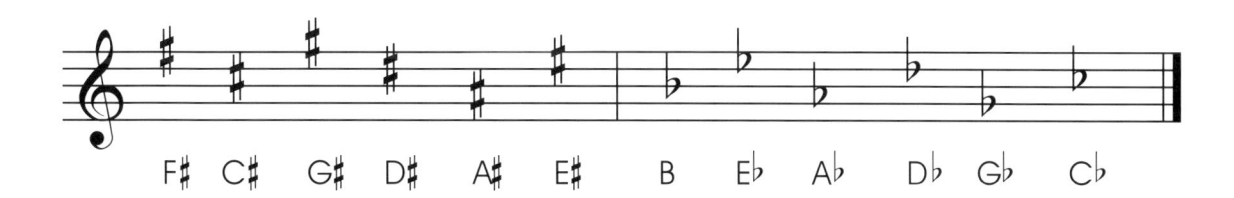

THE MINOR SCALES

Every major scale has a parallel minor scale, which comprises of the same tones and the same accidentals. We find these by going three semitone steps down from the major basic note (from C major to A minor).

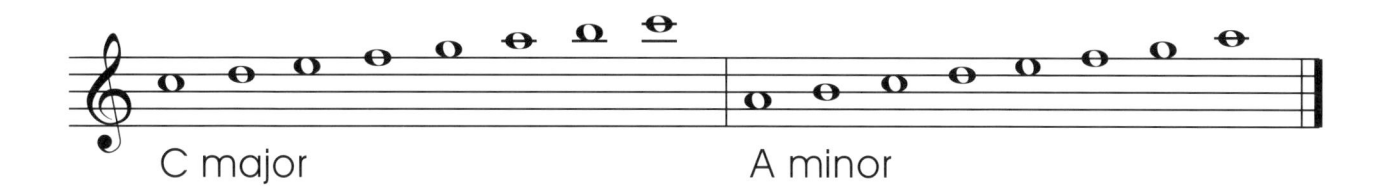

The resulting scales are known either as **Aeolian**, **natural** or **pure minor scales**.
We also recognise the **harmonic minor**, in which the 7th step is raised, and the **melodic minor**. In the melodic minor the 6th and 7th steps are both raised on the way up through the scale, but lowered again on the way down.

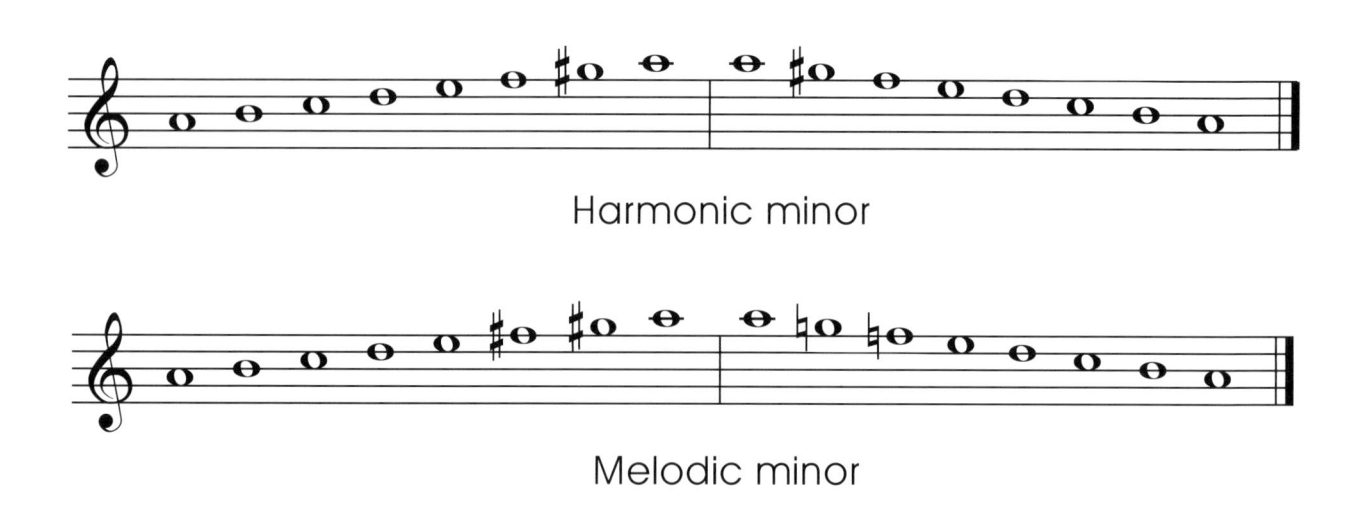

Harmonic minor

Melodic minor

THE MINOR CIRCLE OF FIFTHS

As with the parallel major keys, the minor keys can also be presented in a circle of fifths.

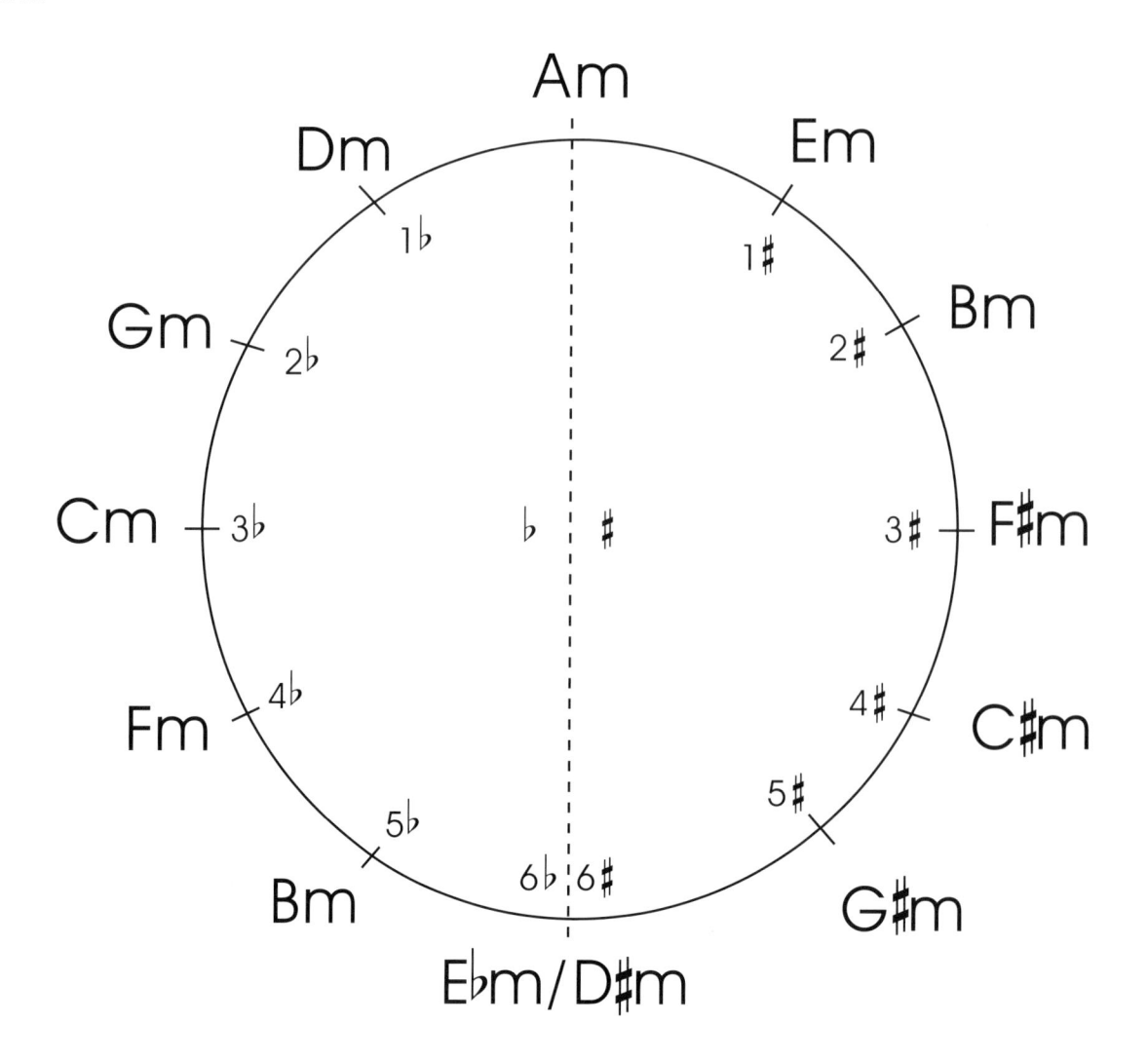

THE CHORDS

INTERVALS

If we wish to know something about the creation of the chords or harmonies then we must first look at the distances or pitch separations between the tones within a scale. The distance between 2 tones is called an **interval**.

The intervals are known by the following names:

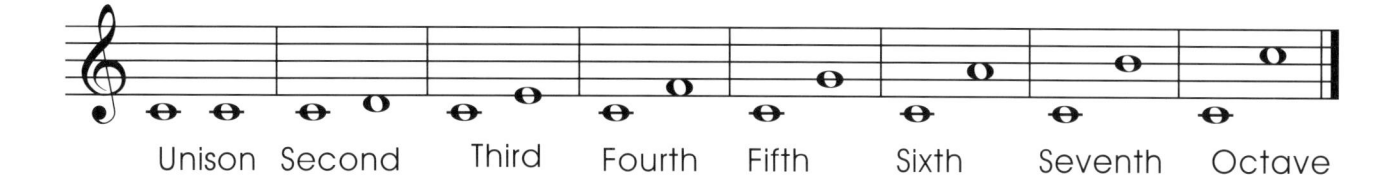

Unison Second Third Fourth Fifth Sixth Seventh Octave

The names indicate the specific tone on the major scale (unison = the first tone, second = the second tone, etc).
We differentiate between **perfect** intervals, and **augmented** and **diminished** intervals. Perfect intervals only exist in this form. These are Unison, Fourth, Fifth and Octave.
The other intervals can either be augmented or diminished: Second, Third, Sixth, Seventh.

THE TRITONE

Tri-tones are intervals which span three whole tones.
The octave is divided into two equal units.

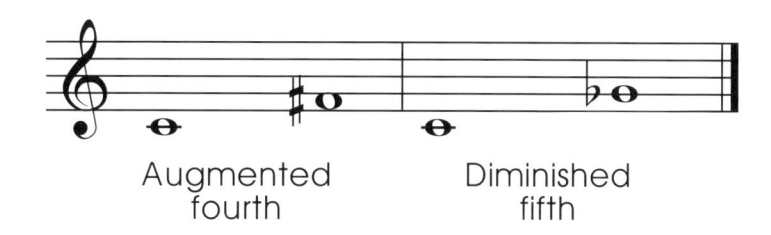

Augmented fourth   Diminished fifth

ENHARMONIC EXCHANGE

Enharmonic refers to two notes which are written in different ways but which sound the same. Determining whether the same tone must be written as F♯ or G♭ depends upon the context (interval) or the relationship with a specific key. This exchanging of note names with the aid of the ♯ and ♭ signs is known as an **enharmonic exchange**.

CHORD CONSTRUCTION

The sound made by three or more notes played together is called a **chord**. The laws of chord construction are based upon an understanding of harmony. The most simple chords are the **triads** (comprising of three tones). These are created using the **first** (root), **third** and **fifth** notes of the scale.

In the case of a **major triad**, the chord comprises of the basic note, a major third and then a minor third.

In a **minor triad** the order is reversed. First comes the minor third, then the major third. In both major and minor triads the interval from the root to the top note is always a fifth.

The **diminished triad** includes 2 minor thirds, whilst the **augmented triad** includes 2 major thirds.
In the case of a diminished triad the interval from the root to the top note is a diminished fourth (tritone), whilst an augmented triad spans an augmented fifth from root to top note.

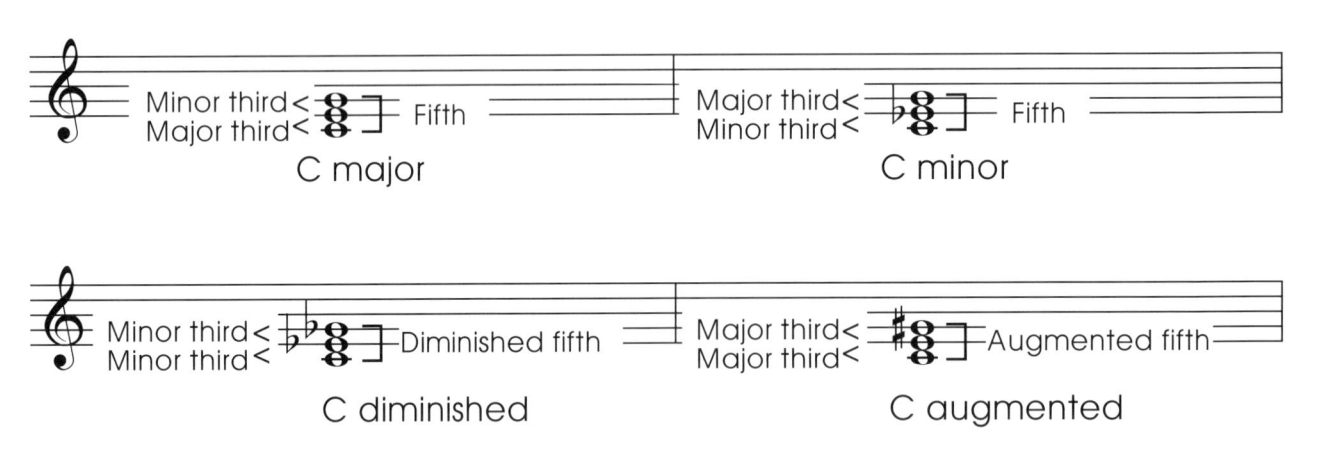

Every key includes three primary triads, which are built on the first, fourth and fifth note of the scale (also called scale steps).
These are called the **tonic** (1st step), **subdominant** (4th step) and **dominant** (5th step) chords. The minor triads on the second, third and sixth steps are called the secondary triads.

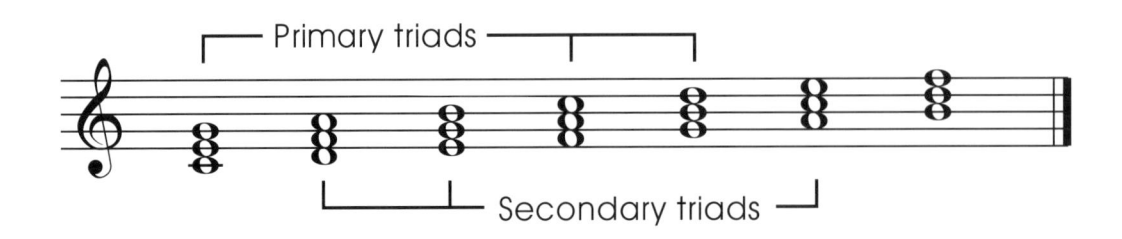

Attention: In the case of the minor keys the triad on the fifth tone step is always the same as a major chord (see harmonic minor).

CHORD INVERSIONS

All triads can be twice inverted. In addition to their **root position**, in which the root note is the lowest note in the chord, there is also the **first inversion** (root note is at the top of the chord) and the second inversion (the root note is in the middle). In order to invert a chord one simply moves the bottom note up one octave.
The **first inversion** is also known as a **sixth chord** due to the distance of a sixth between the lowest note and the basic note.
The **second inversion** is also known as a **six-four chord** (the distance between the lowest note and the basic note is a fourth, the distance from the lowest note to the highest is a sixth).

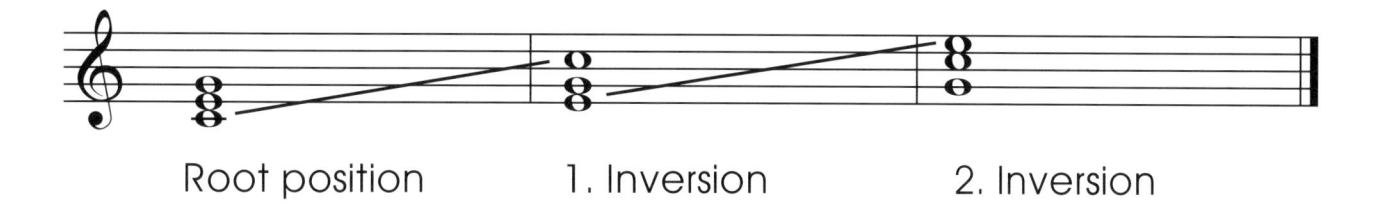

Root position   1. Inversion   2. Inversion

THE SEVENTH CHORD

A seventh chord is constructed by adding an additional third to the triad. Particularly common is the seventh chord built on the 5th scale step (the dominant) of the major scale. This chord is called a **dominant seventh chord**.
The major third is followed by two minor thirds in this chord.

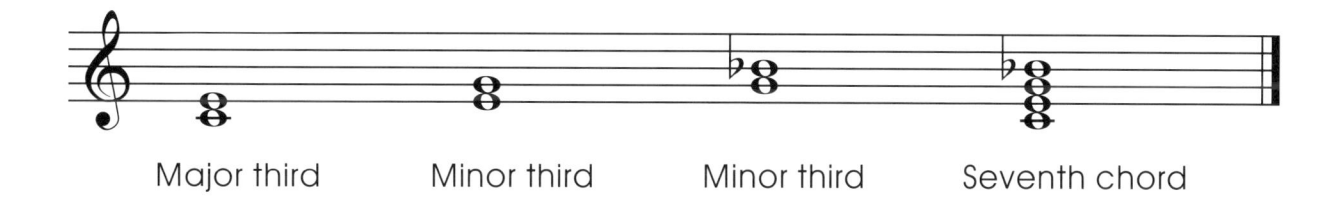

Major third   Minor third   Minor third   Seventh chord

The **minor seventh** chord comprises of a minor third, a major third and one further minor third.

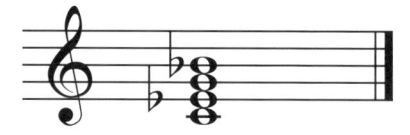

Minor seventh chord

A seventh chord can also be constructed from a diminished chord, with the aid of an additional minor third. The **diminished seventh chord** can be derived from the dominant seventh chord by flattening the top three notes. In this way the top note appears to have been flattened twice, resulting in a diminished seven. This double flattening of a note is usually enharmonically exchanged for easier reading.

Diminished seventh chord

If one adds a major third to the basic major or minor chords then one constructs a chord known as the major 7 chord.

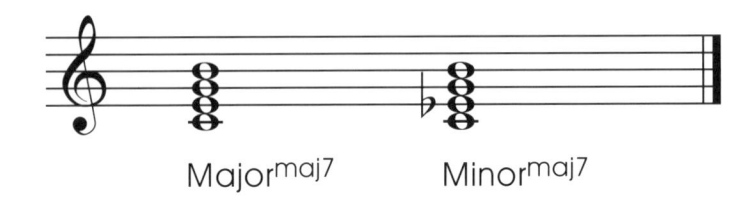

Major^{maj7}   Minor^{maj7}

THE CHORD NAMES

In order to avoid writing out the notes for each chord every time, we instead use **chord symbols**.

The **capital letter** informs the musician of the basic chord note. If it stands alone then this is a major triad chord, below for example we have a **C** for **C Major**.

The addition of a small **m** indicates that the triad is a **minor triad**, here for example **Cm**, for **C Minor**.

C   Cm

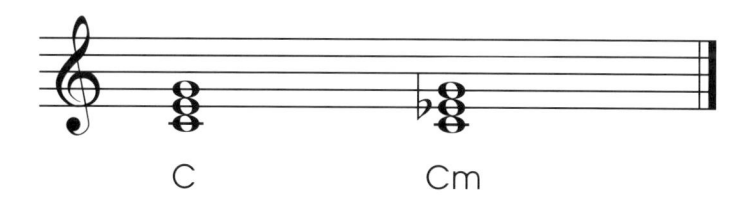

Diminished triads are symbolised by a superscript **0** (zero), whilst **augmented triads** are indicated with a superscript **+** (plus).

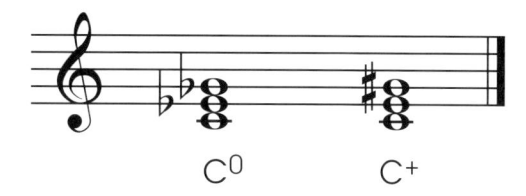

C^0 C^+

The seventh chord with a minor third added to the basic chord is symbolised by a superscript **7**, whilst the seventh chord with a major third added to the basic chord is symbolised by a superscript **maj7**.

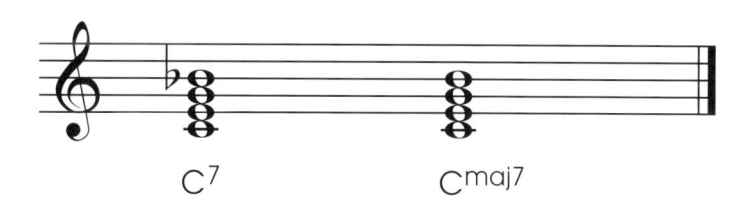

C^7 C^{maj7}

The diminished seventh chord which comprises of three minor thirds is indicated with a superscript **07**.

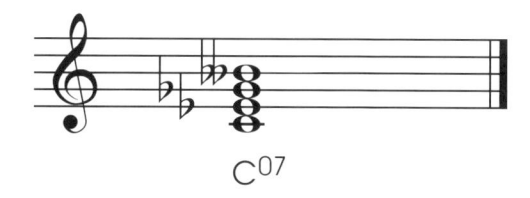

C^{07}

If the sixth tone of the scale is added to the chord then this is represented by a superscript **6**.

C^6

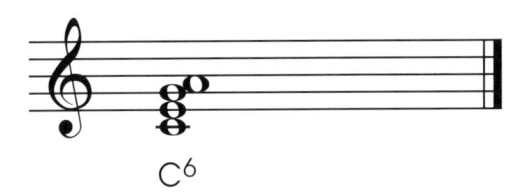

In chords which include a fourth, all of which are major chords, the third note is replaced by the fourth. These chords are indicated by the addition of **sus4** (meaning suspended fourth) after the chord symbol.

C^{sus4}

CD-Tracklist

Track	Titel	Page
1	JOSHUA FIT THE BATTLE OF JERICHO	12
2	WHAT SHALL WE DO WITH THE DRUNKEN SAILOR	13
3	ADVENTURE IS STILL CALLING	14
4	WAKING UP IN WONDERLAND	15
5	GO DOWN, MOSES	15
6	SWING LOW, SWEET CHARIOT	15
7	CORINNA	17
8	MY BONNIE IS OVER THE OCEAN	17
9	IT´S ME, OH LORD	18
10	SHE´LL BE COMIN´ ROUND THE MOUNTAIN	20
11	SOMETIMES I FEEL LIKE A MOTHERLESS CHILD	21
12	BACKWATER BLUES	22
13	HOUSE OF THE RISING SUN	23
14	THE FIRE IN YOUR EYES	26
15	The Riff from the song MAKE ME MOVE	27
16	EXERCISE 1	30
17	EXERCISE 2	30
18	EXERCISE 3	30
19	EXERCISE 4 (notes on the g string)	31
20	EXERCISE 5 (notes on the b string)	31
21	EXERCISE 6 (notes on the g and b strings)	31
22	OH, WHEN THE SAINTS	32
23	EXERCISE 7 (notes on the e string)	32
24	EXERCISE 8 (notes on the g, b and e strings)	33
25	DOWN IN THE VALLEY	33
26	EXERCISE 9 (notes on the d string)	34
27	EXERCISE 10 (notes on the a string)	34
28	EXERCISE 11 (notes on the d and a strings)	34
29	I CAN´T BELIEVE IT	35
30	EXERCISE 12 (notes on the e string)	35
31	EXERCISE 13 (notes on the d, a, and e strings)	36
32	TOM DOOLEY	36
33	JOHN BROWN´S BODY	36
34	TABULATURE CONVERSION	38
35	STRUMMING PRACTISE	39
36	STRUMMING TECHNIQUE IN 3/4 TIME	39
37	STRUMMING TECHNIQUE IN 4/4 TIME	40
38	STRUMMING TECHNIQUE IN 6/8 TIME	40

CHORD DIAGRAMS

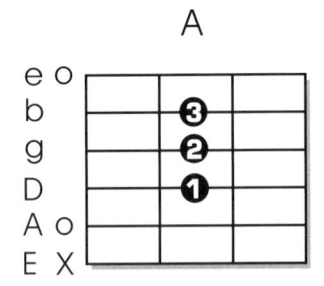

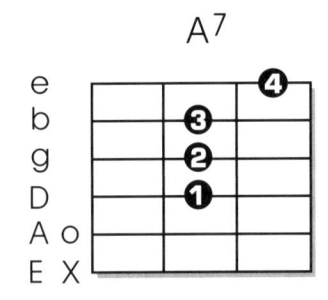

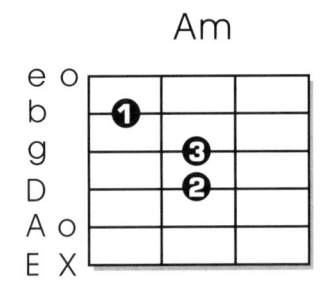

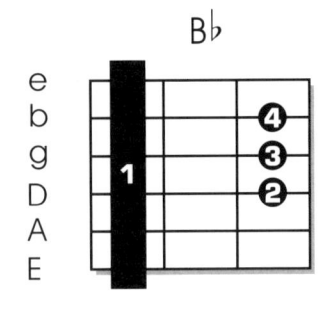

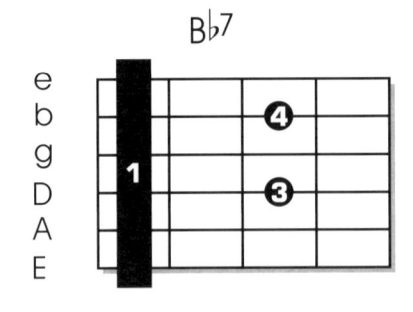

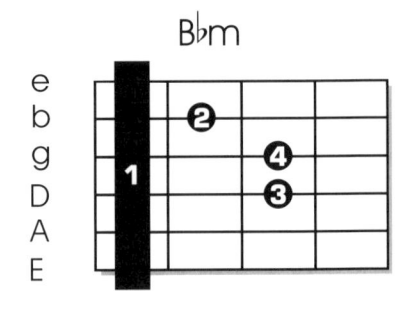

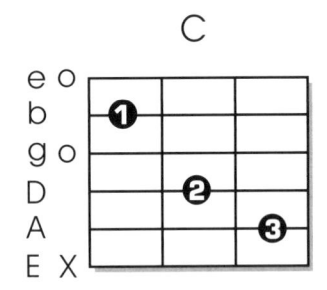

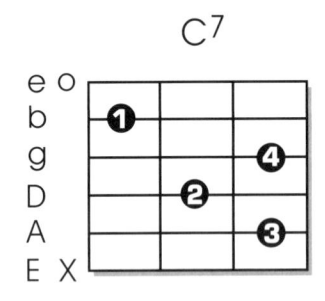

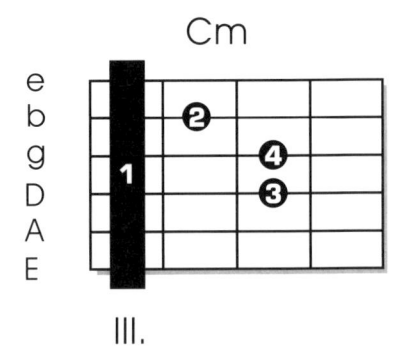

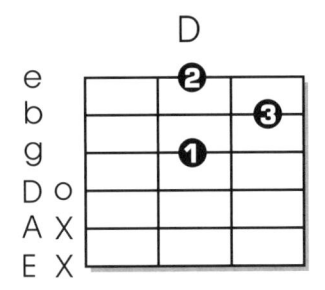

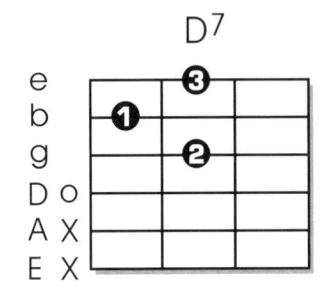

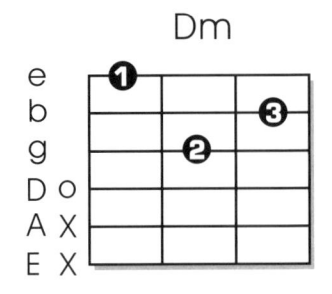

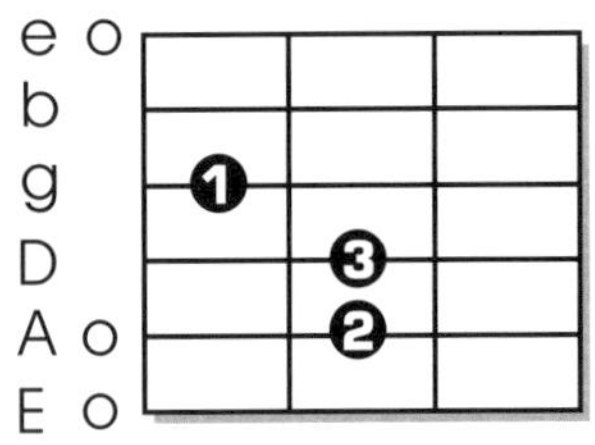

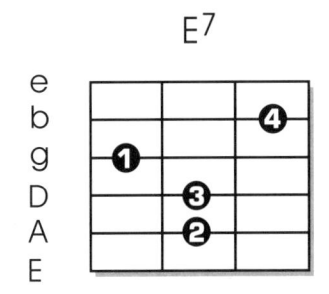

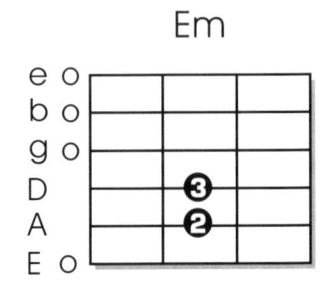

F

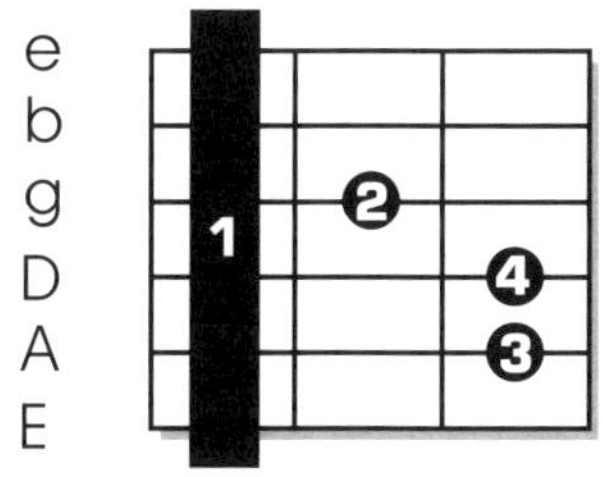

F^7

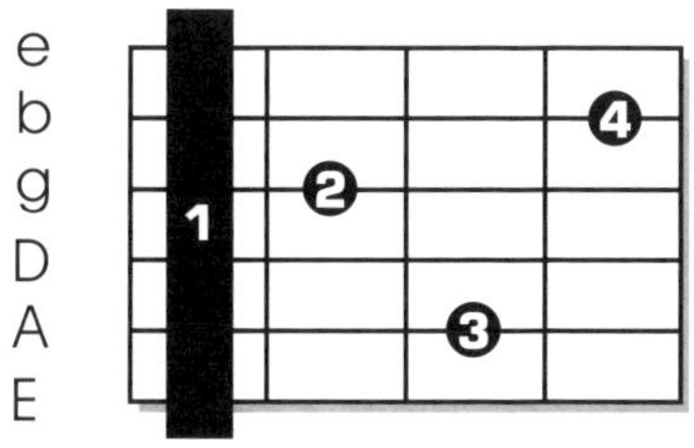

Fm

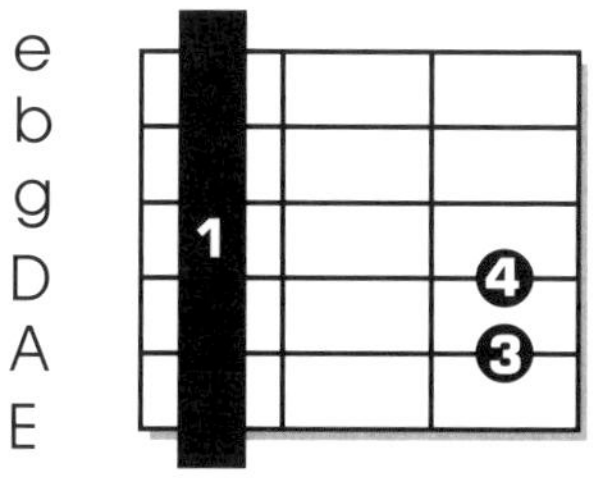

G

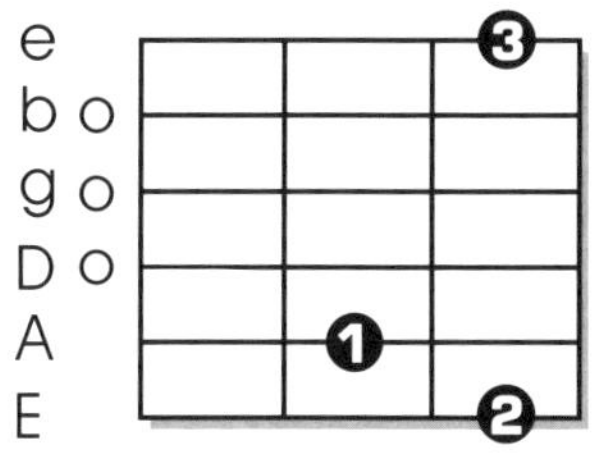

G^7

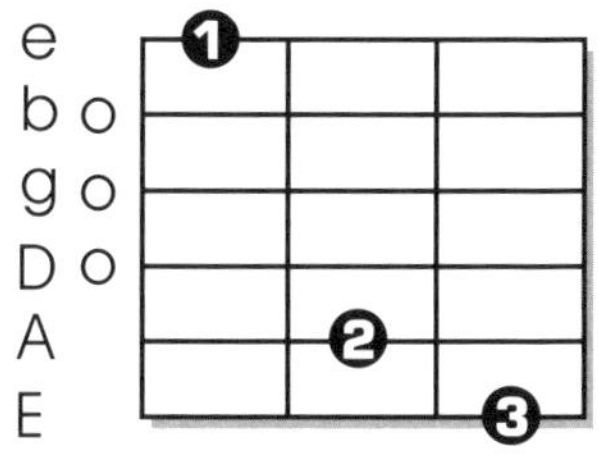

Gm

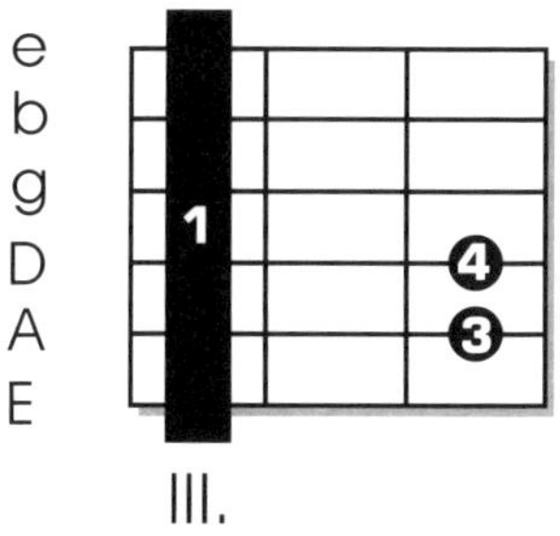

B

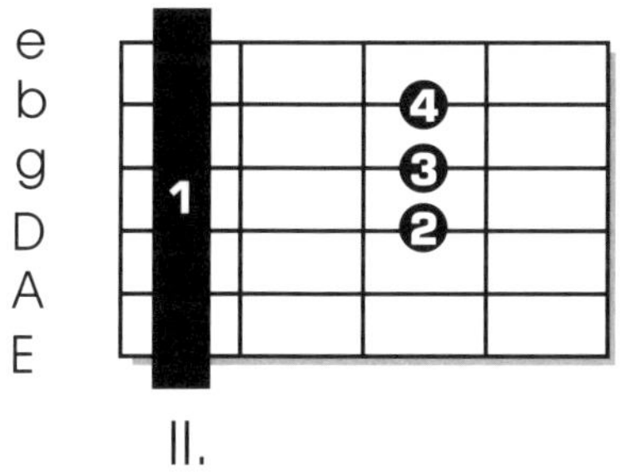

B^7

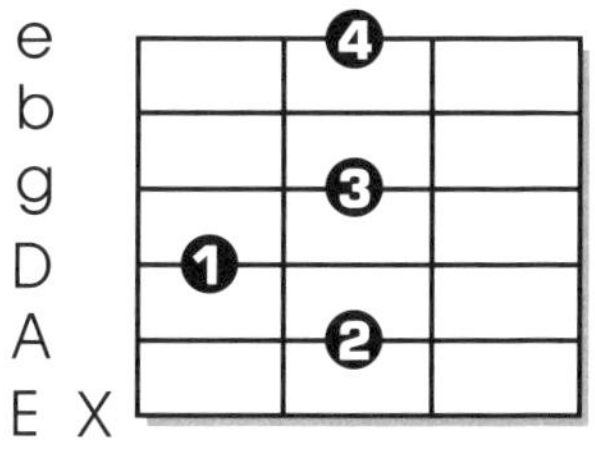

Bm

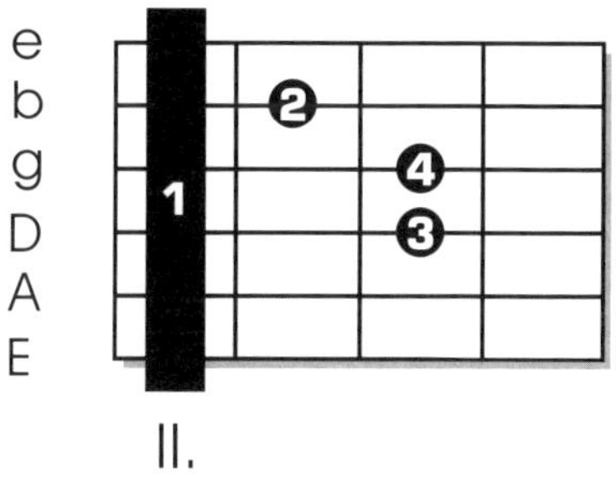

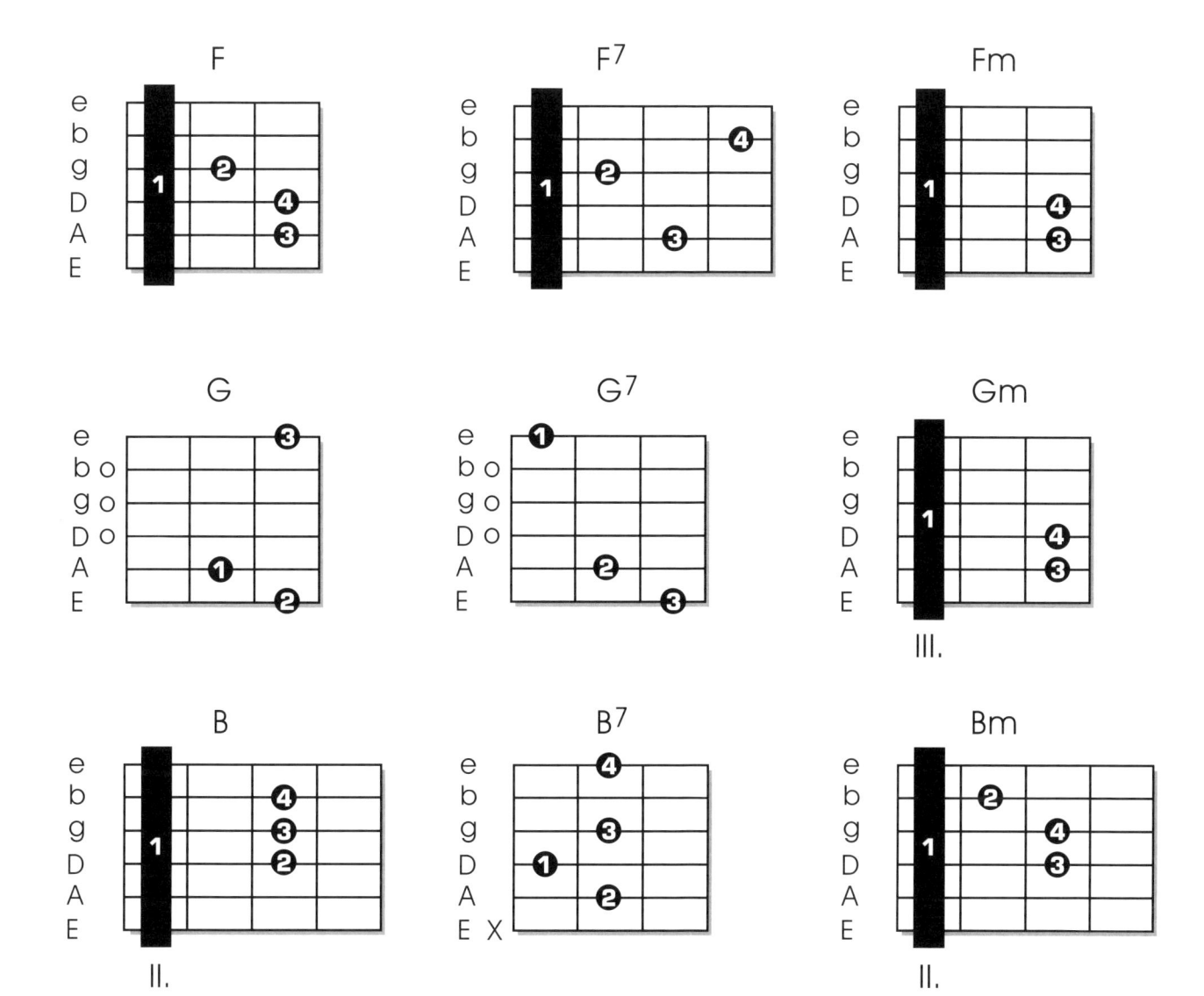

www.voggenreiter.de

www.voggenreiter.de